MASS CULTURE

-N8-

MASS CULTURE

EUCHARIST AND MISSION IN A POST-MODERN WORLD

Edited by Pete Ward

Published by
The Bible Reading Fellowship
Peter's Way, Sandy Lane West
Oxford OX4 5HG
ISBN 1 84101 069 3

First published 1999
10 9 8 7 6 5 4 3 2 1 0

Acknowledgments
Scripture quotations designated NJB are taken from The
New Jerusalem Bible, copyright © 1985 by Darton,
Longman & Todd Ltd and Doubleday & Company, Inc.
Scripture quotations designated NRSV are taken from
The New Revised Standard Version of the Bible,
Anglicized Edition, copyright © 1989, 1995 by the
Division of Christian Education of the National Council
of the Churches of Christ in the United States of
America, and are used by permission. All rights reserved.
Scripture quotations designated REB are taken from the
Revised English Bible with the Apocrypha, copyright ©
1989 by Oxford University Press and Cambridge
University Press.

A catalogue record for this book is available from the
British Library

Printed and bound in Great Britain by
Caledonian Book Manufacturing International, Glasgow

CONTENTS

ABOUT THE CONTRIBUTORS

Jonny Baker is Director of Youth for Christ in London. He is part of Grace, an alternative worship community in West London, and this is the context in which he has developed the ideas in his chapter. He is also chair of Brainstormers, which provides training in youth ministry.

Stephen Cottrell is a missioner with Springboard, the Archbishops' Initiative for Evangelism. Before this he was Diocesan Missioner for the Diocese of Wakefield. He is one of the authors of *Emmaus* (National Society/Church House, 1998) and has written several other books, including *Praying Through Life* (Church House, 1998). He is married, has three boys and lives in Huddersfield.

Graham Cray is Principal of Ridley Hall theological college in Cambridge. He was vicar of St Michael-le-Belfrey, York, for fourteen years, and has a special interest in mission to post-modern culture.

Sam Richards is Director of Oxford Youth Works and Course Director for the Oxford Centre for Youth Ministry, juggling training Christian youth workers with supporting young mums. She is passionate about rugby, chocolate, Dave, and young people having the opportunity to encounter Jesus and the kingdom of God.

Mike Riddell is a writer, teacher and storyteller based in New Zealand and currently lecturing at the University of Otago in Dunedin. A former Baptist pastor turned Catholic layman, Mike has many years' involvement in the alternative worship movement.

Dave Roberts is Managing Editor of *Worship Together* magazine, and is the Director of the Worship Together conference programme. He attends an independent charismatic church in Eastbourne and is the first non-conformist editor of the influential charismatic monthly *Renewal*.

Pete Ward is Lecturer in Youth Ministry and Theological Education at King's College, London. His books include *Growing up Evangelical* (SPCK, 1996) and *Youthwork and the Mission of God* (SPCK, 1997).

ESSENTIALLY STRANGE: COMMUNION AND CULTURE

Pete Ward

'And the other thing I'm doing is a book about culture and the communion service. It's called *Mass Culture*—get it?' No, he didn't get it. 'So why are you bothering with that?' my friend asked with a mixture of puzzlement and disdain.

This was one of my regular catch-up meetings with a youth-work friend of mine. We meet from time to time to share how our lives are going. This time we were in a pub just down the road from my office. I had been talking about the things I had on the boil at that present moment and I suppose I had saved my most exciting new project (this book) until the end. The problem was, my friend wasn't impressed, he just couldn't get his head round it. 'So why are you bothering with that?' I was outraged; could he not see how important the communion was for outreach in our culture? But then why should he? What evidence is there that the communion service makes a difference in practice to youthwork—or any other kind of Christian mission?

My friend had a point, and I had to admit that it was the accuracy of what he said that made me angry. This only partly explains my reaction, though. I was also deeply frustrated that somehow the Church had managed to take the central act of Christian worship—communion—and disconnect it from people like my friend. Surely communion, of all things, should feed mission and evangelism? If communion was not connecting with young people, surely something was badly wrong?

This was a brief flashpoint in a conversation, but I have recounted it here because I think it highlights why, at this time, a book about communion and how it relates to present-day culture is very much needed.

THE HEART OF THE MATTER

A brief tour round a Christian bookshop is very revealing. There are plenty of books that deal with the worship of the Church, and many of these discuss at some length the practice and theology of communion. There are increasing numbers of books that explore the issues of the gospels and ones that explore contemporary/post-modern culture. There are, however, very few books that bring these two areas of thought together. This is the idea behind *Mass Culture*. The aim is to start a discussion about the relationship between mission, contemporary culture and communion.

The contributors to this book have been chosen because they come from different theological and Church traditions, but they were also selected because they share a concern for mission in contemporary society. Their original brief was very basic: write about the relationship between communion, mission, and present-day culture. The result is this collection of original and creative reflections on the worship and mission of the Church. Despite the differences between the authors, their contributions demonstrate a convergence of opinion. The result is that a number of broad themes emerge throughout the book.

That the themes recur in the contributions is less than surprising—communion has generally been close to the heart of Christian identity and worship throughout Church history. We may come from a variety of Church traditions or hold different theologies dear, but somehow communion connects us with the gospels in a way that goes beyond our differences. Added to this, while the commitment to the practice of outreach and mission may vary for each of us, we are fairly close in our appreciation of the effect that contemporary culture has upon these activities. If I am honest, I invited a number of the authors to write contributions for this book because of the similarity of their views on these matters. Yet, what I have discovered as I have read these chapters, is that questions of mission and culture seem to be concentrated or magnified when they are considered in relation to the theology and practice of communion. Somehow, it seems that when we take mission, culture and communion seriously, a number of issues are brought sharply into focus and the creative sparks start to fly. I have summarized the discussion, as I see it, under the following three headings.

The captivity of Church culture

Talk of communion leads to a realization that churches seem to have a culture that is all their own. The confusion over the name—Lord's supper, eucharist, mass, breaking of bread—is a good indication of how particular we are about how we practise communion and how we interpret our practice. (Incidentally, I have opted to use the word 'communion' in this book because it seems to me to be the most accessible term.)

Whatever our particular theology, I suspect that most Christians feel that communion is 'special'. We express this in a variety of different ways. Mike Riddell and Jonny Baker in their chapters recognize the special place that communion has for most churchgoers, but they object to the way that this then leads to restricted access. Mike Riddell calls this the 'fencing of the table', that there is a tendency to keep away both unbelievers and those outside a particular denomination. The belief that communion is someway special or important often seems to work against mission. The 'specialness' of communion, however, is also expressed by the variety of ways that churches 'do' communion.

Communion at its most basic is a very simple act involving the recounting of an incident in the life of Christ and the eating of bread and drinking of wine. Christians have developed a number of complex traditions connected with this ritual. These involve the use of music, styles of clerical dress, ritual actions, the architecture and arrangement of places of worship, patterns of words or liturgy that are generally said and so on. These various traditions are an indication of the importance of communion for the life of the Church, both past and present.

However, the problem—as nearly every writer in this collection points out—is that these traditions, while they may be very highly regarded by Church members and leaders, are, in general, unrelated to contemporary culture. Communion comes across as a remnant of some past age. It *is* old and venerable, we know it is important and for many of us it is spiritually powerful, but it is also frustrating. The Church tradition around communion often seems to dislocate us from our contemporary culture. Thus we are faced with the irony (or maybe the blasphemy) that communion, which is meant to speak both of Christ's giving of himself for the world, and to demonstrate the inclusive nature of the Christian Church, often alienates unbelievers and sometimes fails to communicate gospel grace. Moreover, for committed Christians, it seems to locate encounter with the divine in a cultural environment that is alien to the one in which most of us live our lives.

These are serious issues, and they lead the writers in this

book to express, in fairly strong terms, the absolute necessity of bringing about change in the way we do communion. Jonny Baker speaks of the need to 'reclaim' the rite, Stephen Cottrell of the need to 'reinvigorate' the eucharist and Sam Richards of the importance of 'communicating the story'.

There is a widespread and growing realization that the music, ritual, organization, texts and practices of our churches are out of touch with the mainstream of contemporary culture. This is far from new—most theologians and cultural commentators writing from a Christian perspective would echo this kind of opinion. At the same time, it seems that the way we do communion seems extraordinarily resistant to change. Communion, perhaps more than any other act of worship, is held captive in a conservative Church culture. The authors in this book agree that it is precisely this that needs to be changed if mission in contemporary culture is to succeed. They also recognize that the traditions and liturgies associated with communion have succeeded in keeping the Christian community connected to gospel truth.

What is needed therefore is a contextualization of communion within contemporary culture that remains connected to the residue of gospel truth seen in the tradition of the Church. This involves a balancing act, and it is much easier to be successful when writing a book about it than when working with a real congregation. Yet, despite its difficulties, it remains a basic goal of Christian mission and worship.

COMMUNION IS ESSENTIAL FOR MISSION

Communion recounts and makes present the gospel of Jesus Christ. Stephen Cottrell and Graham Cray, in particular, explore the theology of communion and describe how it encapsulates the Christian story in both word and action. They also make clear that it is precisely because communion is rooted in a gospel encounter with Christ that it is of such crucial importance for mission. Theologically, it is inconceivable that communion should bear no relation to mission. If it relates to mission, then it must connect, in some way, with contemporary culture. Of course, the current practice of the Church may not be connected in this way, but it does not mean that this kind of dislocation is either desirable or necessary.

It is insights like these that lie behind the increasing number of experiments in worship among young people and other groups within the Church. As Jonny Baker and Mike Riddell make clear, the primary motivation within what some call 'alternative worship' has *not* been to change worship so that it will attract outsiders into the Church. Rather, the idea has generally been for Christians, who, on a day-to-day basis, consume and appreciate contemporary culture, to try to make sense of Christian worship for themselves. They do this by using popular forms of music, video technology, ritual and community life. This is seen as being mission-based, because it is a genuine interaction with the cultural climate of our media-oriented world. At the same time, there is a realization that whatever kind of worship emerges will inevitably communicate more widely.

Communion has been a source of inspiration and experimentation for many within 'alternative worship'. The mixture of symbol, story and ritual that make up the rite have been very fruitful for those seeking new ways to connect contemporary culture and worship. Communion, however, also brings the theological and spiritual weight of Church tradition into play in a unique way. There is a sense that, if worship can incorporate a sensitivity to a changing, diverse, post-modern culture and, at the same time, celebrate communion in a way that is recognizable to believers and non-believers alike, then something significant has been achieved.

At the other end of the spectrum from alternative worship

are those charismatic groups that have also developed their own styles of worship. Dave Roberts explains that charismatic spirituality has embraced a worship style based on spontaneous expression and freedom in worship. However, he also shows how charismatic worship can have a tendency to become routine and somewhat stylized. He describes how, in recent years among many charismatic groups, there has been a growing appreciation for tradition and liturgy. A concern to integrate communion with these new patterns of charismatic worship has played a key role in bringing this about.

Charismatic worship, in its desire for relevance and immediacy in worship, has always been linked to mission. The aim has been to see churches as more lively and open places that welcome outsiders. Yet, even in this context, communion has been difficult to ignore. The communion holds within it extraordinary resources for encounter with God, and it is this aspect that charismatics find impossible to ignore.

COMMUNION AND THE GOSPEL

Communion is a repository of Christian tradition and theological truth. The desire to reach out in ways that connect with those outside the Church is extremely important. At the same time, as we do so, there is always the danger that we may let go of apects of the gospel in our desire to be relevant and in touch with those outside the Church. Culture is made *by* people *for* people. It will therefore have aspects of it that work, and are in tune, with Christian faith, and there will be aspects of it that limit the action of the gospel. Contemporary culture or postmodernity is no different in this respect.

Many within the Church experience contemporary culture as a fundamental challenge to the faith. The conservative, enclosed nature of the worship of the Church is a response to the challenge of post-modernity. It offers a retreat into a safe, homey environment that promises us, while outside everything may be unsteady and rapidly changing, at least in the Church we know where we are. The problem, as many of the contributors to this book point out, is that when we retreat we also seem to lose something of the heart of what the gospel is all about. This is brought into sharp focus by the communion service.

Retreat into a Church culture disconnected from the world in which we live is extremely beguiling. Viewed from within, it is very hard to make a distinction between the gospel and the church's own particular cultural expression of the faith. When we abandon the attempt to contextualize the faith in contemporary life, we lose the ability to sift what is a gospel rejection of a particular aspect of culture from a defensive reactionary position that grows from our cultural dislocation. As a result, many of the Church's responses to post-modernity are simply a defence of Church culture.

If communion is to be reframed within contemporary culture, it must be done in a way that is true to the gospel—that is, a way that does not do damage to the nature of communion itself. Graham Cray makes this point with some force. His argument, in brief, is that much of what has been put forward as 'post-modernism' is incompatible with Christian commitment. A post-modernist communion is a contradiction in terms. Post-modernism speaks of the end of all meaning, grand narrative and truth. Communion, on the other hand, points to a God who is 'beneath the surface', the author of the Gospel story and the source of all truth. At the same time, while we may not necessarily advocate post-modernism, we all live in a world that is experiencing post-modernity. How can we celebrate a communion that is rooted in the gospel without selling out to post-modernism? This is precisely the dilemma *Mass Culture* is trying to grapple with, and the chapters that follow offer insights and examples of some ways forward.

YOUTH CULTURE:

IN IT BUT NOT OF IT

Many of the recent innovations in worship have been influenced by youth culture. This is very much the case for the charismatic styles of praise and celebration. In both of these contexts Christians have wrestled with the theology and practice of communion. They have done so, however, out of a worship that has been contextualized within an aspect of contemporary popular culture. Since the 1960s Christian young people have tried to develop styles of worship using the music that has been popular at the time. The widespread adoption of new musical forms for worship has brought with it a significant sea change in the culture of many of our churches.

Change has come about because large sections of the Christian community have been anxious to be 'relevant' to young people. Reaching out to a younger generation has usually been accompanied by the adoption of a youth 'style'. With the clothes and the music has come a way of being Christian that has been reshaped by this 'contextualization' within popular culture. As the gospel has come alive for young people it has found a means of expression within popular culture. The contemporary Christian scene has therefore been forged from a creative interaction between the gospel and the forms and conventions associated with popular culture. The result has been that a growing number of festivals, record companies and media offer the contemporary Christian a fusion religious culture (or cultures). Worship has been central to these developments.

The reshaping of religious life in the form of popular culture has not been imposed on a reluctant public. Far from it. The consumption of a religious culture depends on the active and enthusiastic participation of consumers. We buy the CDs, go to the festivals and bring home the T-shirts. This is not just a commercial activity, it is linked to our sense of religious belonging. Young Christians use the products of a Christian popular culture as sources of identity and meaning. Who we are as Christians has become linked to the kind of worship songs we sing and what festivals we go to.

The contextualization of the gospel within popular culture is, in my view, a cause for celebration. Without the energetic and creative activity associated with the production and consumption of religious media, the Church would be a much sadder and, I fear, deader place. However, as a result, we appear to have hitched our cart to the whirlwind world of popular culture and this has brought with it significant problems.

Popular culture is not a static entity—it is continuously and rapidly changing and extremely varied. The way that young people construct their social identities in relation to contemporary media has undergone significant changes in the last fifteen or so years. The nature of the media has reacted to this shift by developing more diverse and varied incarnations. With Christian life so closely associated with the mores of popular culture, these changes are starting to have a profound effect on young Christians as they consume religious products allied to this culture.

In my view, this is where the practice and theology of communion can be brought into play. Where so much is on the move, maybe communion can represent a point of orientation and stability for a contextualized Christian popular culture. The Christian youth worship scene has been concerned to be 'relevant' and accessible in contemporary culture, but, as the authors in this book point out, relevance must not be pursued at the expense of faithfulness to the gospel. The gospel speaks of a God who is above and beyond our human expressions and limitations. This means that our worship should be both an expression of faith within culture and an attempt to point beyond culture. God, of course, meets us where we are, in the words, music, bread and wine. All of these are made by human hands and are therefore 'cultural'. At the same time, an encounter with the living God within culture reminds us of our mortality and limitations. The word I want to use for this is de-contextualization.

De-contextualization is what happens when a young person from the inner city climbs a mountain in Wales for the very first time. De-contextualization is what happens when a charismatic evangelical Christian visits a Catholic shrine such as Lourdes and they feel the familiar touch of the Spirit. De-contextualization, therefore, is an experience that jolts us out of our current way of seeing and doing things. Suddenly we look at life in a different way. It is my view that communion carries within it an ever-present possibility for de-contextualization. Communion is strange, wild and holy. This does not arise from what we do, it comes from God.

A NATURAL MOVE:
CONTEXTUALIZATION
IN YOUTH CULTURE

A glimpse of God, who transcends culture, is urgently needed at this time. The reason for this is that we have been very successful in expressing the faith within youth culture—so much so that it seems natural to many of us that our worship should reflect the contemporary styles of music. In the late 1990s the existence of vibrant and creative Christian popular culture can seem quite natural—it's part of the way things are. In the early 1960s, however, very little of what we recognize as youth-oriented Christianity existed. The story of how the Christian music scene came about and then how it was able to colonize the wider Church is beyond the scope of this present chapter.

There are, however, four main points that can be highlighted to demonstrate the natural move towards popular culture.

MUSIC ATTRACTS

Evangelism was the motivating force in the developing relationship between evangelicalism and popular culture. Christians believed that pop music would attract young people and bring them to faith. It is interesting to observe that, from this essentially theological concept, an economic and social reality was born. This was inevitable. Youth culture exists in the relationship between the production of records, clothes, films and so on and their creative consumption by groups of young people. Identity and consuming are integrally linked.

YOUTH CULTURE IS LIFESTYLE

Towards the end of the 1960s in San Francisco and other parts of the United States young people who had been involved in the counter-culture began to turn to the Christian faith. The result was a combination of relatively conservative faith with the sub-cultural style of the hippies: the Jesus Movement was born. What was an indigenous youth movement in the US was imported to the UK as a consumer package and the appropriation of popular culture became not simply a strategy for evangelism, it also offered the possibility of a new, and of course 'hip', way of being Christian.

For many Christian leaders, the new Jesus Revolution was a wonderful work of God. Writing in 1971, Michael Green heralded the faith of these young Christians:

I encountered the Jesus People in Australia this summer and rejoiced in their vitality and zeal. There are various groupings of young Christians in their teens and twenties (of whom the Jesus People are one) who have dedicated themselves to a wholehearted, world-renouncing Christianity, and live in communes marked by deep mutual fellowship and love, together with a burning evangelistic zeal. [1]

Green saw much to admire in the commitment of these young people and the way that they found new ways to express the faith and evangelism. Green was critical of the adult Church, characterizing their faith as 'domesticated' and comfortable. In contrast, he welcomed the commitment of these new young Christians.

Similar sentiments were expressed by Billy Graham in his book *The Jesus Generation*:

I have become convinced that the 'Jesus Revolution' is making a profound impact on the youth of America and shows signs of spreading to other countries. One thing is certain: Jesus Christ can no longer be ignored!' [2]

Many were able to look beyond the hippie style and music of the Jesus Movement and see the possibilities for a radical new kind of discipleship. Christian leaders such as Michael Green, Billy Graham and many others saw in the commitment of these young people a fulfilment of their own hopes for the Christian Church. Here were young people who were full of joy in their worship, enthusiastic in evangelism and willing to sacrifice a great deal to be a part of 'God's great plan'. While conservative religious leaders may have appeared a million miles away from hippie music or their dress sense, they were willing to tolerate these for the sake of the gospel. The contextualization of the gospel in youth culture was born out of this bargain.

THE CHARISMATIC MOVEMENT

The style of the Jesus Movement and charismatic worship became closely interconnected in Great Britain. One of the ways in which this changed the indigenous Christian scene was that the use of rock and folk music as an evangelistic tool was slowly eclipsed by the growth in praise and worship music. The trend was started by Jimmy and Carol Owens' musical *Come Together*. The album, which was promoted by a tour featuring singer Pat Boone and charismatic leader Jean Darnell, sold more copies than any other Christian recording during the decade.

Worship music was suddenly centre stage and several artists were able to (re)launch careers in this specific area, most notably Graham Kendrick. In Kendrick we see the potent effects of merging popular music and charismatic spirituality. His impact on the worship scene can only really be understood in relation to the increasing popularity of festivals, celebrations, worship music available from record companies, religious publishing and so on. The mushrooming of such activities indicates a healthy market where producers of religious culture find that they are able to sell to a public eager to buy. Thus, the current worship scene is integrally linked to the enthusiasm of Christians for the consumption of a gospel contextualized in the cultural forms of popular culture.

Young People Grow Up

What started as a youth thing very soon colonized the majority of mainstream churches. There is a very simple reason for this —young people grow up. Within fifteen years or so the young people who were first part of the Jesus Movement were themselves the leaders of churches and Christian organizations. As the 1970s gave way to the 1980s, it was clear that the entrepreneurial activities of a few key players had transformed the Christian world in this country. As Richard Branson and Anita Roddick are to the high street, Graham Kendrick, Gerald Coates and Clive Calver are to the Christian counter-culture scene. The simple process of ageing meant that the Christian youth culture was brought into the heart of the Church—it was a natural development.

THE PROBLEM WITH YOUTH

CULTURE

The contextualization of the gospel in the youth culture of the 1960s and 1970s was a natural development for the Christian Church. The pay-off was fairly clear. Young Christians got a hip new style and the Church saw enthusiastic, committed disciples. This basic deal was at the heart of Christian work among young people then and has continued to the present day.

The effect of this arrangement has been the creation of an increasingly attractive and creative Christian cultural scene. Through record companies, publishers, marketing, festivals and so on, Christian young people have been offered, and have created for themselves, an ever more sophisticated subcultural world. This 'scene' has tended to present itself, and be used by young people themselves, as an alternative to mainstream youth culture. As this has happened, so the sense of belonging and identity that is usually associated with youth culture was merged with particular understandings of Christian lifestyle and discipleship. These developments have been so successful that the newly constructed Christian scene has been able to represent itself as an all-embracing religious world where Christians can find a sense of identity, meaning and belonging. A consequence of these developments has been that, over the last thirty years, Christian commitment has become associated with participation in this scene. To be an enthusiastic young Christian, it has been necessary to be familiar with particular festivals, worship music and so on.

Alongside the promotion of Christian subculture, there was disapproval of the wider secular scene. This was such that, within some Christian circles, it was common for the consumption of 'secular music' to be discouraged or even denounced. Youth culture during the 1970s was constructed around well-defined, tight-knit groups. These groups held in common strictly defined dress codes and tastes in music. Christian belonging was also tightly defined by patterns of activity and music. In this way, the scene worked in roughly the same manner as any other youth culture at that time. There was a logical fit between the sense of identity and belonging associated with most youth cultures and the evangelical commitment of many of those involved in the Christian subculture. A conservative gospel could therefore become articulated with this aspect of youth culture in such a way as to ensure commitment and Church membership. Tight boundaries and a strong sense of belonging meant that those involved in the Christian youth scene could fulfil their theological ambitions.

The way that this was played out in the lives of young Christians can be illustrated in the development of Greenbelt. One of the main concerns of those involved in Greenbelt has been the exploration of the relationship between Christianity and the arts. In effect, what this has meant is that the festival has been at one and the same time a showcase for Christian artists and an arena for debate about the wider secular scene. Discussion, and the artistic policy of the festival's organizers, has revolved around notions of two different artistic worlds. This division or sense of a boundary (even if it was kicked against or argued away) grew from an evangelical inclination towards a separatist theology, but it was given life by the exclusivity inherent in the social dynamics of the youth culture of the 1970s and early 1980s. The one is contextualized in the other.

Greenbelt's cultural sensibilities emerged from the tensions and contradictions experienced by young Christians who were socialized into the Christian cultural scene. For many, the worship and artistic activity that originated from the alliance between youth culture and evangelical Christianity was a lifeline and something to be celebrated. At the same time the Christian scene created problems in its exclusivity. From the very beginning there were those who were more interested in getting into the secular music scene and those who were opposed to such ventures. Some were critical of what they saw as substandard Christian music and favoured a more open attitude to artistic life outside the strictly defined Christian field. This debate has been with us for almost thirty years now, but there are signs that it is losing its momentum and, in part, this is because of changes in the way that young people consume cultural products.

At the end of the 1990s it is clear that youth culture has become a much more varied environment. Contemporary youth culture or, more properly, cultures, are characterized by increasing diversity and fragmentation. The effect of this has been to break down the strong collective identities that had existed among many young people. Where once there were mods and rockers or skinheads and hairies, there are now so many different groups and subgroups that it is almost impossible to make any generalization about styles of dress, musical tastes, behaviour, values and so on. In fact, the only generalization that can be made is that no generalizations are possible!

One aspect of this is that young people's tastes in music have become very hard to predict. The prevailing wisdom is that young people's identity is rarely to be found in a close identification with particular styles of music or individual groups. The response of record companies to the changing youth scene has been to offer a diversity of different bands and artists packaged in a seemingly endless variety. The youth market is fragmented, fast-changing and very fickle. At the same time, the popular music scene has been characterized by a much more rapid turnover of songs and acts. One example of this is that, while more singles than ever are being sold, a large number of records leap very rapidly into the charts and then sink without trace in a matter of a week or two. The change in the music business reflects, and is influenced by, changes in the way that young people construct their identities. In place of easily identified youth groupings, young people now seem to be much more chameleon-like in the way that they consume styles of dress, behaviour and music. Identity is therefore created from a number of different and diverse sources. Personal style and taste is put together from a variety of contrasting media influences. Consequently, allegiance to any one artist, style of dress or social environment is much looser than was previously the case.

The effect of these changes on the Christian youth scene has been quite profound. Young people appear to consume the Christian scene in roughly the same way that they consume other scenes. That is, they move from one to the other fairly easily and construct their identities from whatever takes their fancy. The exclusivity that characterized both youth culture and the Christian youth culture in the last few decades has largely collapsed. The effect of this has been that many Christian young people have ceased to experience the tensions that character-ized the sensibilities and debates of the previous (Greenbelt) generation. The competing demands of Christian and secular scenes have lost their power because the cultural logic of con-temporary culture is that no scene is exclusive.

This basic shift in popular culture impacts the contextualiza-tion of the gospel in popular culture in three key ways.

• Young people are less likely to be embarrassed by the poor quality of music or recording or performance in the Christ-ian scene. Instead, they treat it as part of the show. Christian dance music, worship music and so on are taken for what they are and, on the whole, they love it.

- The enthusiasm of many young people for the contemporary Christian scene is deceptive to those familiar with the earlier dynamic within youth culture. Those Christian leaders who are comfortable with the exclusive Christian culture interpret this enthusiasm as success, but those who are inclined to be critical of a separatist mentality are highly critical of festivals such as Soul Survivor.

- Ironically, both groups are probably mistaken. It is more likely to be the case that young people attracted to the Christian scene are simultaneously consuming a variety of other scenes.

This change in the way that young people consume Christian youth culture has far-reaching implications for the construction of identity, belief systems and belonging. The assumption on which most Christian youth leaders continue to operate is that involvement in Christian youth culture will have a profound and lasting effect on young people's lives. The exclusive claims of the Christian popular culture are built on the natural contextualization of Christian discipleship with a high level of participation in the scene. This connection was very successful —once.

The problem is that, in the current environment, such activity in the Christian scene does not necessarily ensure identification with a Christian lifestyle or a system of belief. Enthusiasm for worship or Christian music or attendance at festivals does not necessarily bring with it significant investment of identity and belonging in the way it seems to have done in the 1960s or 1970s. Christian young people are much more likely to follow their peers, dipping into various scenes, and, as a result, they are more culturally nomadic than in the past.

DISCIPLESHIP FOR NOMADS

The changes in the way that young people consume youth scenes are both a challenge and an opportunity for the contextualization of the gospel in popular culture. It is a challenge because the articulation of Christian lifestyle and the consumption of a Christian subculture have been disconnected. This means that while young people may assimilate much of the Christian message as a result of their involvement in Christian popular culture, at the same time their identity is not totally invested in such consumption. For those of us who are concerned to see young people develop coherent and lifelong Christian commitment, this is a problem. Where at one time a high level of involvement and enthusiasm for the Christian youth scene would have been an assurance of success, this is no longer the case. Young people migrate much more easily from one social arena to another and it is a matter of concern that Christian commitment may not travel with them in the same way that it did previously. In short, while they are at a youth festival, celebration or youth congregation they take on the Christian lifestyle. This lifestyle may not have the same draw on their lives when they are outside the Christian circle. Of course, this has always been the case, but previously there was a sense of loyalty or commitment to the Christian scene and, through that, to the Christian gospel. In the present dynamic of youth identity formation, however, such commitment is likely to be much less clear and, consequently, less enduring.

The nomadic tendency of contemporary young people is, ironically, an opportunity for the Christian Church. For previous generations, the Christian scene was effectively a social and cultural barrier that acted to set them apart from their peers and the wider youth culture. This worked against real outreach and witness. While those involved in the scene tried to make it more attractive and engaging, many young people drawn into its world found that they were disabled in their evangelistic efforts because of their sense of cultural schizophrenia. Young people currently involved in the Christian scene are much less self-conscious about any division. They are comfortable with both a vibrant Christian culture and the wider youth culture. This means that they are much more able to reach out to non-Christian friends than were young people in the past because they inhabit similar cultural worlds. The problem is the extent to which they are able to transport their faith, which is very much alive in the Christian cultural scene, with them as they journey. The successful contextualization of the gospel in youth culture means that many young people have experienced an invigorating encounter with the gospel. The problem is that this faith is in danger of being associated only with the active consumption of that culture. Contextualized expressions of the faith are problematical when they become 'absolute'—that is, where the cultural expression of the faith becomes too closely linked with faith itself.

THE EUCHARIST AS ESSENTIAL

DE-CONTEXTUALIZATION

The Christian gospel must be expressed within culture—otherwise it doesn't come alive. At the same time, the reality of God and the gospel of Jesus Christ are always transcendent of any cultural expression of the faith, however powerful or relevant or inspired that expression may appear to be. The contextualization of the faith within popular culture is also subject to this basic theological reality. The answer to both the challenge and opportunities associated with the present dynamic lies in a renewed appreciation of the nature of God and of the gospel. It is my belief that we can find this appreciation in the communion service.

The development of the Christian youth scene has been driven by the desire to express the faith in terms of the culture of young people. This has been a necessary endeavour and its benefits are evident in the numbers of young people attracted to festivals such as Soul Survivor and Greenbelt and in the way in which many have embraced the Christian life as their own. The contextualizing imperative is deeply felt, but it is my contention that the way that young people consume such culture now demands a parallel and complementary approach: contextualization needs to be complemented by de-contextualization.

De-contextualization is the attempt to grasp a vision of the God who transcends culture and of a Christ who can be incarnate in a variety of historical and cultural contexts. Alongside the vivid expression of the gospel within contemporary youth culture there is a need to offer the Christian gospel as an overarching story. Within the Christian youth scene there needs to be a concern to find ways to present Christ as Lord of all life. Following Christ is a coherent act of everyday living, not just an aspect of participation in one scene among many others. For previous generations of young people, this theological truth was expressed in the exclusive claims of the Christian youth culture. Being Christian was about close identification with the scene. As we have seen, this social dynamic is rapidly collapsing as young people participate in a number of scenes. The need is for the gospel to be presented in a way that is portable, a faith that endures both within and outside of the youth scene. This faith is most powerfully presented in the bread and the wine of communion.

Experimentation with eucharist worship has characterized much of the alternative worship scene. These kinds of services have used all kinds of different music and visuals in an attempt to express the Christian gospel within new cultural forms. My observation, however, is that even in the most successful of services, the ritualistic act of eating bread and drinking wine seems to jar. We might be grooving to the most hip drum and bass track or quietly passing round the elements in an informal circle or gazing at an array of incredible images that form the backdrop to the service, but still the act seems strange. The strangeness is itself cultural, but can be used to our advantage.

Communion holds within it the central narrative of the Christian faith: 'This is my body', 'This is my blood', 'Christ has died, Christ is risen, Christ will come again.' The bread and wine and the simple words that go with them offer an insight into the transcendent nature of God and the over-arching story that shapes us as believers.

Communion has been the central act of Christian worship for precisely this reason. It connects us with Christ, but it also affirms our solidarity with all Christians, past and present and future. In other words, despite our attempts to contextualize our worship in culture, communion points us beyond our present context. It relativizes our best efforts to be relevant. On one level this is of course cultural, as is all human activity. Communion, however, witnesses to the gospel of Christ in a way that is not limited by our creativity, rituals or even our theology. Communion pulls us up short; it transports us into another realm—the kingdom of God.

CONCLUSION

The Christian youth scene is extremely important to the future of the Church. It is vital that every effort be made to continue to connect with young people within their own cultural worlds. At the same time, there needs to be a recognition that this in itself is no longer enough. Those involved with young people need to know that they construct their social worlds in significantly different ways to those of us from previous generations. This means that there is a crucial need for attention to be paid, within the youth scene, to de-contextualizing moments. These moments will, in effect, speak of a God who is bigger than our scene. The most important resource for this is communion.

1

RHYTHM OF THE MASSES

Jonny Baker

Dancing to a new expression
Of an ancient rhythm
Singing out a new song
In praise to the name of the Lord. [1]

WHERE I'M COMING FROM

I have my own story, from which perspective I have a take, an angle, a slant, a telling of the story of God, particularly as re-enacted and told in the eucharist. I prefer to begin by letting you know where I am coming from so you can understand something of the lens through which I see. I am white, English, male, well off from a global perspective, married and a dad. I have grown up in a Christian family, I've known God for as long as I can remember and have always attended Anglican churches. Charismatic renewal and evangelical belief have shaped my faith and experience of God. I have always believed that the story of God is worth sharing with others and work for Youth for Christ to this end.

In recent years I've questioned many of the assumptions behind, and the culture of, the expressions of faith I grew up with and find myself more 'at home' in many ways outside the Church than in it. I have experienced the Church as increasingly irrelevant to the culture I live in, which frustrates me no end as I am still committed to following Christ and being part of his people.

I have found a home in Grace, a community in West London that is part of St Mary's Anglican church. I guess if you were to label it, it would be 'alternative worship', though I dislike the label as it seems to me that what goes on in most churches is alternative to the discourse most people understand in our culture. In Grace I have found a place to breathe and be with God and develop worship that feels authentic, that catches the imagination.

We draw strength and ideas from many places in the Christian tradition, the scriptures, our own creativity and from contemporary culture. This is the arena in which I have 'played' with the eucharist and in which it has come alive for me in ways I never imagined. I make no great claims for my take on the story, though my intuition is that it rings true and hopefully is getting somewhere near the story of God—I certainly don't want to absolutize my telling of it. I hope that as I hear others' stories around the table with Christ my own telling will be subverted, enriched, reworked in such a way that it gets a little closer to the story. That has certainly been my experience to date.

A STORY

A group of teenagers started hanging around with a youth worker based at an Anglican church in West London. The church is virtually on the high street, which is their 'patch' anyway. They make up a typical urban crowd—restless, joking, forever scrapping, bored, energetic and lethargic in equal measure.

You can guarantee that one or other of them is in trouble with the police at any one time.

Although they started coming into the church, they've got no Church background at all—in fact, you might say they are the most unlikely people to be found in a 'nice' Anglican church. On Sunday evenings they would often come in to the basement and have coffee while the service was going on upstairs. Some of them tried going in to the service. As you'd expect, they didn't last long, got the giggles and had to come out, then generally enjoyed taking the mick out of what went on in the service.

However, the church, to its credit, seemed to cope fairly well with them popping in and out and the young people got to suss out pretty much what went on in a service. Most of the bits they would avoid—notably the supposedly up-to-date choruses and especially the sermon—but the thing that they came in for every time was the eucharist. Somehow it drew them in.

I've been to a service there and it is done with great theatre. It is a modern church with a fantastic sculpture symbolizing the Trinity hanging overhead (though on first sight it looks more like Batman's logo projected in the sky). The communion table is situated in the middle of a round communion rail. When the members of the congregation are invited to receive the bread and wine, they come and kneel at the rail and there is then an opportunity for prayer with a member of the prayer team for anyone who would like it. Several of the young people came forward to receive bread and wine and took it pretty seriously (for them).

After this happened for several weeks in a row, the youth worker sat and discussed with them why the church does the eucharist and what they wanted. The outcome of this conversation was that some of the young people preferred to go up just for a blessing, but others wanted to be open to remember Christ and his presence. After that, they continued to take bread and wine and invariably went to ask for prayer from the prayer team, either for themselves, their friends, their upcoming court case or whatever pressing concerns they had. One week, they had found a pigeon outside with a broken wing and brought that up to the rail and asked that it be prayed for by one of the prayer team at the end. They took it to the RSPCA the next day and later in the week went to check on how it was doing!

This pattern is still continuing twelve months on. They hang around downstairs, having coffee and chatting and miss most of the service. As soon as it is time for the eucharist part, someone lets them know and those who want to come and join in. They receive bread and wine or a blessing and go for prayer. Their experience is one of a sense of peace and being touched by God.

Signs, symbols, images, ritual, drama, stories and experience —these are all part of the discourse or language of our culture. We can read and interpret them. A good telling of a story will catch our imagination. In the church service we have just heard about most of the service isn't talking this language, but when it moves to the eucharist, in this particular church, it is. I suggest that's why this part has caught the young people's imagination and why they're finding themselves drawn in to the story of God.

My own experience of the eucharist was somewhat different. It simply didn't catch my imagination in the same way. As a child, it was something the adults did when children were kept out. Then, after being confirmed at the age of fourteen, I was suddenly allowed to join in with the adults. It was fairly disappointing and I wondered what the fuss was about. The words seemed to go on for ever and were recited parrot fashion. Furthermore, pretty much exactly the same words and the same songs with the same dull tunes were used every week. The whole occasion was very sombre. I got the impression someone had died. Someone *had*, of course, but everyone seemed to have forgotten he was resurrected and present in our midst. It seemed an empty ritual, desperately in need of filling up.[2]

Untouchable rite

This ritual began with Jesus' last meal with his friends before his death. In the context of a Jewish Passover meal, he instituted the bread and cup ceremony. For the first few decades after the resurrection, the disciples continued this practice of eating meals in each others' homes with the eucharist. They referred to it as the 'breaking of bread'.

'Remembering Christ' would have consisted of sharing stories around the meal table—his actions, teaching, death, the surprise when he appeared to them in that room, little incidents, parables he told, times they had laughed and wept together. Having eaten with him after he was raised from the dead, they would have been especially conscious of the presence of the risen Christ with them as they ate, perhaps remembering the many meals they had eaten together.

Along with these meals in the early Christian community (sometimes referred to as agape meals), a eucharist service was celebrated on Sunday mornings.[3] These services were characterized by thanksgiving (*eucharistein*) and joy. Many of the hymns and prayers of the eucharist that are used in the Church today are based very closely on ones dating back to the first 200 years of the Church's history.[4] There is something very exciting about the thought of joining with the thousands of Christians down the centuries who have said similar words and kept alive the dangerous memory of Jesus in their re-enactment of the eucharist, worship and liturgies.

However, by about the year 400, the tone of the eucharist

service seems to have changed dramatically. The overriding experience was one of fear. The table was sealed off and a theology of priest and laity had developed, with only the priest having access to the table. We can see an example of the changes that had occurred in theology in the catechises (lectures given to baptism candidates) of Cyril of Jerusalem (349–386).[5] He regarded the eucharist as a sacrifice, but less of a thanksgiving and more of a propitiation. The consecration of the elements of bread and wine brought about a change of an almost chemical kind. Just touching the sacraments had the power to sanctify. To be in their presence was cause for fear and trembling. Rather than joy, everyone was asking 'am I worthy?' with great emphasis being placed on sinfulness.

By the tenth century, sacramental confession was obligatory before mass. It seems people dreaded the table, afraid of hell!

In the sixteenth century, people knelt and looked down, afraid to even look at the bread and wine. The Church even had to plead with people to take communion at least once a year at Easter. From its origins in a common meal, the eucharist had developed into a fixed service. There was no dialogue about how it was celebrated. It had become an 'untouchable rite'.

There have been various attempts to re-imagine communion or take it back for the people. The Reformation in the sixteenth century was perhaps an inevitable reaction. It was a call back to the Bible—bread and wine was for all, there was more participation, but the emphasis on sacrifice remained. However, the eucharist still tended to be sidelined because people couldn't agree on what it meant or how it should be done.

Anabaptists, Methodists, Brethren, Pentecostals, Anglo-Catholics, alternative worship groups and others have, at various times, reclaimed the eucharist with various emphases. Their courageous stories remain a source of inspiration.

However, in spite of these movements, I contend two things about the eucharist in the Church on the verge of a new millennium. First, many people still experience the eucharist as an untouchable rite and, second, the way that the story is told or the drama is re-enacted largely fails to catch the imagination. (In saying this I realize that I am making a generalization and that there are notable exceptions.)

This raises two pressing questions. Will the rite remain untouchable or can it be reclaimed? How can we re-imagine the eucharist in a way that connects with, or draws people in to, the story of God?

RECLAIMING THE EUCHARIST

What I am proposing in suggesting that the eucharist needs to be reclaimed is not some new splinter group or reforming movement. The history of these is something of a mixed blessing. While they all believed that they were restoring the Church to being true to her 'original message', and in some cases acted as a helpful challenge to the rest of the Church, it hasn't taken too long before their angle on the story has become clear and the usual issues of power, control and institutionalization took over. They can, and often did, become more stuck in the mud than the church that they left in the first place.[6] Tradition is often seen as the enemy by these groups. It is clear that tradition can, and has, twisted the telling of the story, but 'it is also responsible for two thousand years of honing, defining and crystallizing the faith'.[7]

What I am proposing instead is that we see afresh the gift from Christ that the eucharist is and begin to make more of it in our own traditions. Along with baptism, it is one of the principal ways in which the Church has passed on the story and initiated people into Christian life, by our becoming part of Jesus' life, death and resurrection.[8] It needs to be reclaimed, both in newer charismatic churches and in the older institutional churches, which, in different ways, are equally lacking in imagination.

Many churches will create space for different kinds of worship. It is not uncommon for a church to have a youth congregation, all-age worship, a Taizé service or a celebration evening. Within these a fair degree of experimentation takes place. For many Anglicans, it is commonplace for set liturgies to be overlooked for such a service, or to top and tail it with something so that it still 'feels legitimate'. However, people feel very differently about doing the same with communion—it still feels 'untouchable'. Interestingly, this is true within a lot of the newer churches as well as the old. Why not do the same with the eucharist? What is so sacrosanct about it? What are we afraid of?

I have been aware of the apparent untouchability of communion within the Anglican Church for a long time. In Grace, we have pushed to reclaim it and see what happens. Within the boundaries of the Anglican tradition and the parish we are in, we have found enough space to make it our own. We still have a priest present who says the words of institution ('On the night that he was betrayed...': as far as I've worked out, this is the really, really untouchable bit), we still have some sort of liturgy, but we are in the process of applying for licence from the bishop to use other experimental liturgies. And we are introducing other media, prayers, music, symbols, meditation, images and so on, drawing from across the Christian tradition, scripture and contemporary culture to make the story come alive.

I will give an example of one way in which we have 'played' with the eucharist later. The point here is to do with the starting place for this journey we are on of recovering the eucharist in our life together. It simply began with imagination—we no longer imagined the eucharist as untouchable or 'off limits', we wanted to make it our own.

Bringing this about has not happened without there being

some tension and heartache within our church, but the congregation has generally been supportive and rooted for us. It became more of an issue when we were wanting to do a regular eucharist rather than just an occasional one. I realize we could have been given a much harder line on things with less room for manoeuvre, but I still contend that, within all our traditions, there are possibilities open to us, there is space to be found on the edges if nowhere else. As various churches and groups reclaim the eucharist and discover Christ's presence anew within it, this will be a catalyst for others to do the same.

Change is both an exciting opportunity and brings with it a threat in the form of the unknown. For church leaders it is often easiest to settle for the course of least resistance, which tends to be not to change things much. Maggi Dawn has written a very helpful essay entitled 'You have to change to stay the same'.[9] She argues that insisting on using the same form and language in worship is blindness because culture and language are always changing. By keeping things the same, their meaning actually changes over time and becomes irrelevant. The challenge for each of us is to 'engage thoroughly with the ancient tradition and reinterpret it through the culture we now live in'.

Dawn quotes Karl Rahner,[10] whose challenge is similar: accept that every generation and culture interprets the gospel. Then, get on with taking part in your generation's interpretation. To put it another way, 'The gospel must be constantly forwarded to a new address because the recipient is repeatedly changing his/her place of residence'.[11] For some this may sound a bit too risky. What will it look like? Isn't there a danger of losing the plot altogether? How will we judge whether or not our generation's interpretation carries any authority? These are fair questions that are addressed below. However, the alternative is to continue to hold on tightly to the old ways of doing the eucharist and it drifting into becoming more and more of an irrelevance.

The grand narrative and

improvization

Andrew Walker and others have articulated a description of the gospel as the 'grand narrative' or the story of God.[12] Each of the books I have read that outline the central themes or chapters in the grand narrative as they see it do so slightly differently.[13] This simply illustrates the point that there are various tellings of the grand narrative—no one can claim to have the definitive version. Our own take or route through it at any particular time is shaped by a variety of factors—our own perspective, our own context, the scriptures, our understanding of the authors' perspectives and contexts in the scriptures, other tellings we have heard, something new in the narrative we had not noticed before... The longer I go on, the less I feel I know or the more I feel there is to discover. It seems that the playing field or arena within which theology or ideas about God can be knocked around is somewhat bigger than I once thought. Indeed, theology 'brings us to the shores of mystery'.[14] This doesn't in any way mean that we can't know anything. This would be a serious mistake to make. The fact that I'm looking through a lens doesn't mean that there isn't an object that I'm looking at.[15]

N.T. Wright takes this a step further. He suggests that seeing the gospel as drama/story in this way can give us some clues as to how we should then live. He suggests that the grand narrative consists of five acts—the first four being creation, the fall, Israel and Jesus. The writing of the New Testament is, then, the first scene of the fifth act, and it gives hints at how the story is supposed to end with a final kingdom and the renewal of creation. The role of the Church is to improvize the final act up to its conclusion. Wright calls this 'faithful improvization'.[16]

For actors to improvize well, they will need to immerse themselves in the story. Their acting will have to be consistent with the script so far and further the author's intentions. The more faithful an improvization is to the story, the more it could be said to have authority or 'ring true'. No doubt there would be disagreements and some improvizations would lose the plot but 'the extant script would function as a touchstone for evaluating various improvizations'.[17] This means that not just any improvization will do but there is room for a range of interpretations.

The eucharist tells a story, and the way we do the eucharist also tells a story. It tells it in the words that are said and perhaps as much in *how* it is said. It gets to the heart of our Christian worldview and the heart of our telling of the story of God. It is the remembrance of Christ's incarnation, life, death and resurrection and a celebration of his life present with us now.

There are at least two mistaken views of authority and faithfulness to the gospel in the way we have celebrated the eucharist in the past. One view seems to be that if we do things the way they have traditionally been done and use the same words, they will carry authority and be biblical. It is the words that are given particular attention. As I have argued above, keeping these the same actually serves to undermine their meaning and they are in danger of losing their authority over time. This is especially so at the present time when the nature of discourse in our culture has shifted so dramatically. It is no longer word-based. Thus, locating authority in the words is to miss the point. In being so dogmatic about the wording of the story, it has lost its magic. We may think we are telling the story but no one can hear it!

(I should add here that I am not suggesting that the words themselves are unusable in their current form or that there is anything inherently wrong with them. The story at the beginning of the chapter illustrates clearly that they can still work, although I feel it is more the drama, symbolism and ritual that has caught the young people's imagination. Many in the Church who are familiar with the words find them helpful and meaningful, but, equally, there are those for whom this is not the case. The point is simply that we need to recognize the way these words have come to have such authority and to question the validity of that.)

The other view of authority is to locate it in the way that the eucharist was celebrated in the New Testament. This is equally problematical for the simple reason that we live in a very different culture from that experienced in Christ's time and in a foreign land. Once again, the discourse has changed and our challenge is to reinterpret it in our context, not maintain it as it was in first-century Palestine. The Anglican report on youth puts it this way:

> The Incarnation was specific to the culture of first-century Palestine, not as a limitation but as a demonstration and guarantee that the gospel of Christ could take specific root within each culture and era. [18]

I think that one of the reasons these two views of authority have held sway is that they can fairly easily be controlled by those in power. I propose that we need to recover the art of faithful improvization if we are to celebrate the eucharist in ways that stay true to the story of God and catch the imagination in our culture. While this is a bit more complicated an approach to authority and those in power will find it harder to keep tight control (which must surely be a good thing), it will help us find a way through.

REALITY ISN'T WHAT IT USED TO BE

Walter Truett Anderson puts it so well in these words, which are the title of his book (Harper, 1995). Indeed, it's not news any more to say that the world is changing. Many writers have written about the emerging post-modern world and what characterizes it. While there are different analyses, the common thread is that we are definitely witnessing a time of huge cultural transition. 'The story that our culture has told itself for the past two hundred years has lost its power to convince'.[19] This is a story of the Western dream of progress and economic prosperity fuelled by human reason—modernism. I suspect the reason the film *Titanic* was so popular was that it had mythical proportions—the sinking ship symbolized a sinking dream. We simply don't believe that story any more. The cultural mood has changed. It's not yet clear what stories will take the place of the myth of progress. One thing's for sure, though—if you think you have it, don't claim it is the story or you're in trouble. You'll be deconstructed before you can say 'Jean François Lyotard'![20] Just tell it—that's OK because everyone else is allowed to tell their story.

> *In the new environment there is increased freedom for us to recount our story. It will not be the only one told but if it has substance and authenticity, then that may well be communicated to the hearers.* [21]

We inhabit a world of popular culture. We choose what to 'buy into'. We share memories of media moments, and images say more than words. We're suspicious of institutions, especially religious ones. We like being playful and ironic, living with ambiguity and paradox. The world we live in is pluralistic, both local and global, experiential, busy, anxious and lonely, and increasingly urban. We value intuition, friends and want what is real or authentic—and what is virtual. We are sophisticated consumers but don't want to be sold anything, especially a lie. We are cyber-connected and technology-dependent. We are afraid of commitment and responsibility, preferring to watch from the sidelines. We are aware that all is not well with planet Earth. We are hurting and looking for new ways to live.

It is within this context that we must find imaginative ways to tell the story that mean it can be heard.

Where are our candles, smells, and electric bells? Where are our images of light and shade, our music of splendour, our divine dramas, the sacred dance? We have a story but no one can see it. We tell the story but no one can hear it. We have a fundamental problem of communication because we are bound to an anachronistic literary culture.[22]

There's a wonderful book by Tom Beaudoin entitled *Virtual Faith*.[23] The subtitle is 'The irreverent spiritual quest of Generation X'. Writing as an insider of the culture himself (which is a refreshing change—so many critiques are given by those pontificating from a distance), he explores popular culture, fashion, body piercing, music and cyberspace, and discerns a search for meaning and spirituality. I was particularly struck by his description of an irreverent spirituality.

This notion lends itself to being easily misunderstood by the Church, which is, broadly speaking, conservative, rational, polite and sincere, but it is also an example of a way in which we might need to employ a different kind of telling. One group I know used a video sequence from the film *The Last Temptation of Christ* as 'wallpaper for the soul'[24] during the eucharist. The sequence has a lamb being slaughtered, a cup of blood carried by a priest, Christ on the cross and Christ breaking bread all looped together. Use of a controversial film would be seen as irreverent by many, but in the discourse of the culture, this kind of telling works wonderfully well. Similarly, an image we have used in a Grace eucharist is of Jesus surrounded by gay men in leathers. It's quite a shocking image (enough for the Pope to cancel his visit to the Swedish Lutheran church that was displaying the material)[25] and again irreverent, but plays well, begging the question who would Christ have shared his table with?

For a culture suspicious of anyone selling them anything, in our telling it will not do to press people to buy into our story. It will simply push them away. This sounds to some like a sell-out and perhaps surprising from someone who works for Youth for Christ, an evangelistic organization. However, we must choose carefully the mode of speech we use and then simply trust the power of the story and its author to do their work.

John Tinsley, in an essay entitled 'Tell it slant',[26] suggests that Jesus was a 'prophet of indirect communication'. He was always 'telling it slant', hardly ever making a direct statement about God in his teaching, preferring stories and questions to subvert the world of his listeners. Tinsley quotes an article from *The Sunday Times*:

> *Our most reliable guide to the holy and eternal now is not the man shouting the latest odds at his stall in the marketplace of personalities, but the artist, poet or priest who stands at an individual angle to the traffic-choked highway and looks obliquely into the ravaged and aspiring heart of man. This is the voice for which we must keep an ear in tune.*[27]

In the eucharist, how then shall we tell and re-enact the story?

Walter Brueggemann describes the current situation as being like a flattened world of prose in which we need to hear the speech of the poet:

> *After the engineers, inventors and scientists, after all such control through knowledge, 'finally comes the poet'... perchance comes the power of poetry—shattering, evocative speech that breaks fixed conclusions and presses us towards new, dangerous, imaginative possibilities.*[28]

The Church must seek out her poets and artists, film-makers, liturgists, painters, musicians, photographers, sculptors and storytellers, recover her imagination, filling up an empty ritual to tell the story again.

PLAYING WITH THE RITE

There is great scope for creativity in celebrating the eucharist. As we grasp more fully the range of meanings in it, we will become a freer and more innovative people. This is a call, in a sense to play with the rite. We will find ways to clothe it in its proper range of stories, to interpret it visually, in gesture and in music. We will ask it questions, learning how to express eucharist through the distinctive language of our culture.[29]

Play is a useful metaphor for thinking about worship in contemporary culture or subcultures and the way creativity can be brought to bear upon it. 'Worship can be seen as the explicitly religious form of play.'[30]

For some, this will sound too light an approach for something as important as worship, but as well as being serious it should be fun. Pete Ward points out the seriousness and cautiousness attached to the process of liturgical revision in the Church of England as it tries to eliminate risk.[31] In this kind of process the most imaginative offerings for new liturgy tend to be filtered out. In contrast, worship as play frees us to be imaginative, to try things out and see how they feel, to take risks, and if we get it wrong, then we can laugh about it together and learn from our mistake to do it better or differently next time.

The experience of many alternative worship groups is that the process of putting worship together is as valuable as the actual service itself. The process of discussing ideas, drawing together the raw materials to work from, going away and creatively and prayerfully writing a song or filming a video sequence, finding some music tracks to use, feels somehow charged with the presence of God before we even get to the service. As we practise we will get better at it, as with any craft.

Returning to the theme of improvization, the best musical improvizers are well versed in their scales, chord structures and musical theory, which gives them the freedom within which to play. The best acting improvization is done by those who know the plot, the author, the characters, the setting, and have developed the skill of acting—it gives them the freedom to play.

The scriptures, the breadth of the Christian tradition, its creeds, theology and spirituality, our own imagination and contemporary culture are the raw materials with which we can play with the rite. If we stay hooked into these, seek to be open to the Spirit of God, follow Christ, and have relationships of support and accountability, we'll stay on the playing field. But, as with music and acting, we do well to be immersed within the story of God before we get too sophisticated in our improvization and play. (It may be that within our particular local church and denomination the parameters for the playing field are drawn a bit more narrowly, but the principle remains the same.) Tom Beaudoin uses the term 'bricolage' for this kind of play, describing worshippers therefore as 'bricoleurs', who can 'recycle and recombine not only the present pop culture and religious landscape but also the rich past of religious tradition'.[32]

There are some wonderful examples of ways in which the eucharist has been played with. Vincent Donavon, a Catholic missionary, describes how he tries not to impose his culture on the Masai tribe he has been sharing the gospel with as they first celebrate communion together.[33] The account is inspiring in the way that they play with the rite using symbols from their culture and in the way that the ritual brings a challenge to their community. Grass is a sacred symbol in their culture and the peace of Christ is shared by passing grass throughout the village. The mass involved the whole village, it wasn't static and was changeable. Masai men had never eaten in the presence of women, not wanting their food to be 'polluted', and it was at the mass that they first ate together, realizing the liberating power of Christ.

The way things are structured and set out—who leads, who distributes bread and wine—have often 'said' that God is authoritarian, male and lives in another world from me. Alternative worship groups in particular have sought to address the symbolism in these rituals. Some groups have said the prayer of consecration together 'in the spirit of the anti-authoritarian Lord'. Most will seek to have a plurality of voices and leaders often not just coming from the front. The use of symbols from our everyday world helps make the connection that 'this is the God that is in my real world, not a God I step out of my world to meet'.[34]

Third Sunday Service (TSS), an alternative worship group in Bristol, have a powerful slide that they use of a Korean reformed pastor breaking bread in front of the barricades of riot police in the student protests just before the collapse of the previous South Korean regime. At Greenbelt '98, each evening Holy Joes led a communion service. One of these evenings, as bread and wine was distributed, The Verve's song 'The drugs don't work' was played. Indeed, many groups have used existing liturgies but had a DJ playing music behind the words, which, while being simple to do, lifts the liturgy in an amazing way.

Those in the St Hilda community have written prayers and liturgies that explore the vision of partnership between men and women.[35]

Sal Solo ran a series called TYME (The Youth Mass Experience), mixing the Catholic mass with icons and contemporary music. When this was led at Greenbelt I was struck by the image of a Catholic priest holding high the elements, praying the prayer of consecration with projections of representations of Christ all round and a young guy rapping to a contemporary tune—it really was ancient and post-modern!

Another group has explored the eucharist in the context of a proper meal, much like the Passover. In Grace, similarly, we have set up tables in a café style to play with the idea of sharing stories round the table with Christ and the theme of hospitality. This played on the image of the Last Supper in the painting by Leonardo da Vinci, begging the question 'Who is invited around the table with Christ?' and, in particular, exploring the challenge of his eating with outsiders.

Some are somewhat sceptical of this process of play. Both Andrew Walker and Tom Wright, for example, while calling for renewal of liturgy, are fairly negative about 'trite and trendy new liturgies'.[36] For others, this process of bricolage sounds exhausting. They want something familiar, with which they can feel secure and safe. I think these concerns are well founded, but my observation of groups experimenting in this way is that they don't end up with something different every week. What they have discovered is that some of the prayers, images, rituals and liturgies that have initially been played with become significant over the long-term in the life of their community. They become part of the corporate vocabulary of worship. As we have explored the theme of hospitality in Grace, for example, this has opened up a new dimension of the eucharist. But many of the ideas have now been crafted into prayers, meditations, video loops, slides and liturgy. What we have arrived at through the process of play is not something trite and trendy (those bits tend to get discarded pretty quickly), but, rather, something fresh, rich, deep and meaningful. Furthermore, it will be used again and again. It is also not unrecognizable for anyone familiar with a liturgical service; after all, we are playing with things that exist in the tradition. We will probably go through a similar process exploring some other eucharistic themes and in this way build up our repertoire.

The most well-known contemporary eucharist was probably the Planetary Mass run by the Nine O'Clock Service (NOS).

While I am aware of the way things went wrong, the service was another inspiring example of reclaiming the eucharist in a way that caught the imagination of many people. We might describe the take on the story of God as one of cosmic redemption. With the gospel reduced to a very individualistic and dualistic telling in many places in the Church, this was, and still is, a much needed telling. As you arrived at the service and walked down, there were images of creation and various quotations. The music, samples played, distribution of bread and wine, and the liturgy took you through a story of the gift of life and creation, told of its destruction and global injustice, confessed our part in that and called us to turn back to God, rediscovering his compassion and resurrection life.

It was a very challenging service. To take part was to be invited 'into a counter-story about God, world, neighbour and self'[37] that would subvert the assumed story in our culture. Many experienced the presence of the risen Christ there.

Another very inspiring take on the eucharist told as the counter-story of the gospel is one of liberation. In his book *The Eucharist and Human Liberation*, the Sri Lankan writer Tissa Balasuriya argues that 'feudalism, capitalism, colonialism, racism, and sexism have all tended to make the eucharist conform to their values and priorities'.[38] The eucharist had so domesticated Jesus that the colonizers and colonized could sit around the table together while the rape of their colonial countries was going on. The way it is re-enacted, rather than carrying its original symbol of liberation, has been about maintaining the status quo.

Balasuriya advocates rediscovering the sharing of bread and all this symbolizes on a global scale, the importance of building radical eucharistic communities and a focus on liberation. This clearly plays well with the original context of the Passover meal and the Israelites' liberation from oppression in Egypt. Have we got the courage to embrace this kind of telling?

A FINAL STORY

Derek Spencer, a youth worker in an Anglican church, was being commissioned by the Bishop of Horsham in September 1998. At the service, in the words of commissioning, the Bishop specifically licensed the youth worker to push the boat out, live on the edges of the Church, experiment with worship, including the eucharist. This is precisely the kind of imagination needed by church leaders to create space for faithful improvization, to enable the eucharist to be reclaimed and re-enacted in a way that will catch the imagination once again. 'Deep within every person is a longing to be connected to a story larger than ourselves'.[39] The eucharist is Christ's gift to us to tell that story and invite them into it.

2

PARABLE AND ENCOUNTER: CELEBRATING THE EUCHARIST TODAY

Stephen Cottrell

If you went in a time machine back to Calvary and stood at the foot of the cross, how would you know that this death is a sacrifice? It would look just like any other execution—after all, human history is soaked in the blood of innocent deaths, and crucifixion was just one of many sophisticated methods for ensuring they would be slow and painful. But for us Christians, this death, the death of Jesus, is the hinge of history. Not another tortured innocent put to the sword, but God's decisive intervention in the human story. How have we reached such a conclusion?

We need to go back further. Back to the night before Jesus died, to the supper he shared with his closest friends. The story of what happened on this night appears in similar versions in the Gospels of Matthew, Mark and Luke, and also in Paul's first letter to the Corinthians (Matthew 26:26–29; Mark 14:22–25; Luke 22:14–20; 1 Corinthians 11:23–27). During this meal, Jesus broke bread and shared it, saying, 'This is my body, given for you'. He then took a cup of wine saying, 'This is my blood of the new covenant, poured out for many for the forgiveness of sins. Do this to remember me.' The Christian Church has always been faithful to this last instruction of Jesus, but what do these words mean?

The Acts of the Apostles refers to the early Christian community breaking bread together (Acts 2:42). Paul's account—probably the earliest—begins, 'For the tradition I received from the Lord and also handed on to you...' (1 Corinthians 11:23, NJB). In other words, even at this early stage, the eucharist was established as a vital part of Christian life.

The Church today also remembers Jesus by breaking bread and sharing wine. We give this meal many different names—the last supper, holy communion, eucharist, mass—but it is what we do that matters. Our celebrations are about a meal shared in remembrance of the Lord and in obedience to his word.

The name I will be using in this chapter is eucharist. It means thanksgiving. It gives us the first clue to the meaning of the eucharist—a thanksgiving meal for all that God has done in Jesus Christ. I think it is the best word to use and it is becoming the most widely accepted across boundaries of denomination and tradition.

What matters, though, is meaning. My intention is to explore the meaning of the eucharist under the headings of parable and encounter; and then to see how this might inform the particular ways we celebrate the eucharist in our churches, especially with children and young people.

An increasing number of churches are growing suspicious of the eucharist. They think it is 'difficult' for people new to faith. We, therefore, need to find ways of rediscovering and reinvigorating the eucharist so it may be what Jesus intended —and what the first Christians experienced—the central act of worship for the Christian Church, Jesus' own way of helping us understand, appropriate and celebrate the harvest of his death.

PARABLE

The last supper was like an acted parable. There are layers of meaning, but, like all the parables, it is not just a matter of extracting the message—Jesus' words always draw us to himself, the living word made flesh.

First of all, Jesus' breaking of the bread and pouring of the wine are prophetic gestures: his body was broken, his blood was shed. The actions at the supper anticipated the death.

It is likely, however, that this meal was part of the Jewish Passover. In which case, the words he spoke, and the dramatic actions with the bread and wine—startling enough in themselves—are charged with the ambience of salvation.

The Passover is the greatest festival of the Jewish year. To this day it is celebrated to remember God's saving action in human history when the people of Israel were liberated from slavery in Egypt. Each household had to slaughter a lamb or goat and smear some of the blood on the door posts and lintel of the house where it was eaten. In this way, when the Lord came to destroy the first born of Egypt he would see the blood on the Israelites' houses and pass over, sparing them. They then left Egypt to be led by God through the desert to the Promised Land. (We can read about this in the book of Exodus.)

This is the context of the last supper. Jesus is not just warning his disciples about his coming death, he is giving them a way of understanding its deepest meaning. Just as the Passover is a sacrificial meal in which the blood of the slaughtered lamb spares those who eat and drink, so Jesus identifies himself as the lamb of God whose body is broken and blood spilled to also bring salvation. It was probably impossible for the disciples to make this connection as they gathered with Jesus in the upper room on that Thursday evening, but, after Jesus' crucifixion, and after they had seen him risen from death, they would remember. In other words, Jesus himself establishes a link between the actions of the last supper and his death on the cross.

The word 'remember' is vital here. Like in the Passover, it is not just concerned with passively recalling a past event; it is an invitation to participate in a living reality. God acts in human history, but he is not confined by human history. The first Christians make the connection—what God achieved in the death and resurrection of Jesus is now made present in sharing bread and wine. 'Do this to remember me' is to be understood in the Passover context as 'do this and I will be with you'. In this way, we understand his saving victory over sin and death as past event, future hope and present reality.

Every human age is equidistant from God's eternity. The astonishing reality of the Christian faith is that God's eternity has indeed broken into human history. A relationship with God is now made possible in a new covenant, established by the blood of Jesus. The breaking of bread and sharing of wine, as Jesus instructed, become the meal of this new covenant, just as the Passover was the meal of the old one.

Through the eucharist we understand the death of Jesus as a sacrifice. Without the eucharist it would be much harder to properly fathom the meaning of his death. And because all this is entrusted to us in a meal, the salvation of the gospel is prevented from being just an abstract proposition about the nature of God—it is given as 'table fellowship' to which every human being is invited. The eucharist is the Christian Passover. Salvation is now offered to everyone.

ENCOUNTER

The eucharist is what the Church calls a sacrament. The most basic meaning of a sacrament is the 'pledge of a covenant'. (In Latin, the word *sacramentum* referred to a soldier's oath of allegiance, which he would make when enlisting.) There are two great sacraments in the Christian faith: baptism and the eucharist. Both of them are pledges of the new covenant that Jesus established between God and humanity. A sacrament is therefore about establishing commitment and relationship. (Thus, marriage has also become one of the seven official sacraments recognized by the Roman Catholic and Orthodox churches. Paul also likens the covenant relationship between Jesus and the Church as being like a marriage (Ephesians 5: 31–32).) However, the important thing about the sacraments is that they communicate what they signify. Thus, the eucharist does not just point the way to God. By sharing in the sacrament of the eucharist God comes to us.

The Christian faith is, by its very nature, sacramental. Through the incarnation the matter of the universe—in this case, the rapidly dividing cells in the womb of Mary—becomes the vehicle for expressing God's grace and truth. We can call Jesus the sacrament of God—God's expression of himself in space and time—in order to know and be known by the world he made. Jesus himself continues this sacramental way of channelling God's presence in his own institution of baptism, as the means of entering into the new relationship with God, and the eucharist, a means of being continually nourished and upheld in that relationship. The *Anglican Book of Common Prayer* has a marvellously succinct definition of the sacramental action: 'an outward and visible sign of an inward and spiritual grace'. The bread and the wine are the outward signs; the inward grace is the receiving of the body and blood of Jesus.

Some people fret over the body and blood language. Indeed, the first Christians were accused of cannibalism. Their defence was simple: we are not feeding on the body and blood of our dead leader; our leader is alive! It is the risen life of Jesus that is communicated in the eucharist.

As well as taking us back to the last supper, the eucharist

transports us forward to the banquet of heaven. Throughout the New Testament, from the great feeding stories in Jesus' ministry to the references in Revelation to the Lord sharing a meal with those who heed his call (Revelation 3:20), the kingdom of God is described as a banquet. The Lord has prepared a place for those who love him (John 14:3) and, by breaking bread and sharing wine, we receive a foretaste of the promise that awaits us. The body and blood refer to the life of Jesus— an eternal life that feeds the human spirit, sustaining us in this life with the life of the world to come. Archbishop David Hope described this as 'remembering the future'. The sacraments enable us to participate in eternity. In which case, the meals we should remember when we receive communion are the meals Jesus shared with his disciples after his resurrection: the breakfast on the beach at the end of John's Gospel (John 21:13); the supper at Emmaus (Luke 24:30).

Eastern Orthodox Christians refer to the eucharist as 'the mystery'. Partly, this is an admission of defeat; no, we do not know how Jesus is present when we share bread and wine (Christian history is stained with the blood spilled from this argument); but we boldly declare that he is not absent.

This, though, is not a mystery that is beyond the bounds of reasonable discourse. We human beings are used to designating value and meaning to material things. We print a certain design on a certain piece of paper and designate it a ten-pound note. Interestingly, we also describe this as a pledge of something else. However, the ten-pound note is not just a symbol; it can actually be spent. It has real currency. So it is with the bread and wine of the eucharist: to say that they become the body and blood of Jesus does not imply a material change. The Anglican–Roman Catholic International Commission, in its 'Elucidation on Eucharistic Doctrine', explained it this way:

God uses the realities of this world to convey the realities of the new creation. Before the Eucharistic prayer, to the question: 'What is

that?', the believer answers: 'It is bread.' After the Eucharistic
prayer, to the same question he answers: 'It is truly the body of
Christ, the Bread of Life.'[1]

So what does all this mean when I kneel at the altar rail, or
stand in a circle, and place that small piece of broken bread in
my mouth? What it means is that I am encountering Jesus. It is
Jesus I am meeting and Jesus I am receiving. He is the host who
invites me to his table. He is the lamb who gave himself that I
might be saved. He is the food and drink of my life. His body
and blood have been given for me.

The account of the last supper in John's Gospel does not
include the institution of the eucharist. He places the action a
day earlier. This is because he wants to tie the death of Jesus
precisely to the moment when the lambs are being slaughtered
for the Passover, thus underlining the point he makes right at
the beginning of his Gospel that Jesus is the Lamb of God (John
1:36). However, he still has high regard for the eucharist. After
feeding the multitude with fish and bread, Jesus makes this
astonishing declaration (John 6:51, 57–58, NJB):

I am the living bread which has come down from heaven.
Anyone who eats this bread will live for ever;
and the bread that I shall give
is my flesh, for the life of the world...
As the living Father sent me
and I draw life from the Father,
so whoever eats me will also draw life from me.
This is the bread which has come down from heaven;
it is not like the bread our ancestors ate:
they are dead,
but anyone who eats this bread will live for ever.

In the eucharist, Jesus has given us a way of understanding his death and a way of receiving his life. This bread is not just food to our stomachs, but food to our souls. This bread is not just a symbol of Jesus; it is a channel for receiving Jesus. When we receive this bread in faith we become what we eat, and through the consecration by the Holy Spirit, Jesus is formed in us; we are renewed as members of his body. As Paul says, 'The bread that we break, is it not communication with the body of Christ?' (1 Corinthians 10:16).

CELEBRATION

The eucharist is a party. From the earliest times to the present day, Christian people have been faithful to Jesus' command: 'Do this to remember me.' But this remembrance is at once solemn—the memorial of passion and death—and joyful— the festival of resurrection. The pattern of the celebration is discerned through the experience of the eucharist as parable and encounter. The celebration of the eucharist is itself an acted parable, telling the story of salvation and recounting the mighty works of God, and, of course, the eucharist is an encounter.

So far, however, we have only concentrated on the sacramental encounter, but the eucharist is more than this. As well as encountering Jesus in bread and wine, he is also to be found in the breaking open of scripture and in the gathering of his people. This threefold encounter is symbolized by the action of the eucharistic liturgy.

In the early Church (and still in many churches today), at the beginning of the eucharist the priest would kiss the altar. This sensual greeting announces to the assembly that this is a place for parable and a place for encounter: an altar connecting us to the sacrifice of the cross; a table where the faithful gather in communion with the Lord. Around the altar we meet Jesus.

Likewise, when the gospel had been read, the deacon would kiss the scriptures, for the same reason. The Bible is not just any book, but God's word, inspiring, rebuking and challenging our lives. Through scripture God spoke to people then and he speaks to us today. Through the scriptures we meet Jesus.

Finally, the people of God were invited to greet each other with a kiss, and this kiss has resurfaced in the new liturgies of recent years. This sharing of the peace of Christ is the great unsung third climax of the eucharist. In the Anglican rite, it comes at a pivotal point between word and sacrament. Having heard Jesus in the scriptures, and in readiness to receive Jesus in the sacrament, we turn to our neighbour and greet the presence of Jesus in each other.

The whole shape of the eucharist is based on these encounters. First the people in the church gather to break open the word of God with readings, exposition, exhortation, prayer and affirmation of faith; there is confession and absolution; there is the sharing of peace. Then the action moves to the altar. Bread and wine are taken, blessed, broken and shared in the same way that Jesus took and blessed and broke and shared the bread and wine at the last supper, and in the same way his own life was offered, blessed, broken and shared for the life of the world. We are then bidden to love and serve the Lord in all we do.

There are, of course, many different forms and many different customs that accompany this celebration, but in virtually all Christian traditions this basic pattern can be discerned. Even the elaborate liturgies of some of the Church's traditions are at heart very simple. Where incense is used, for instance, the three things to be marked out as holy by the act of censing are the altar, the Bible and the gathered Christian community.

In some churches it is still controversial to share peace. It seems all too touchy feely, not very English. Perhaps it has not been properly explained. Sharing peace is not about being nice to one another. It is about belonging to one another as Christ's body (though we are many, we are one body because we all share the one bread). It is a prophetic sign of communion and encounter. As a result of our baptism in Christ, our salvation by his dying and rising, and our participation in his eucharist, we are a new community. The old bonds and the old barriers of kin and class and caste and creed and colour have no reckoning here. I am now received at the banquet of heaven. I need no other affirmation.

Thus, we tend to think about the main action of the eucharist in two parts: the liturgy of the word and the liturgy of the sacrament. This is sometimes described by modern liturgical scholars as the two tables of the Lord. However, I want to highlight a third element—the table fellowship of the people of God. It is our reason for gathering and the momentum that drives us from the Lord's table out to be service to the Lord's world.

Encountering Jesus in the eucharist is not an end in itself. As Bishop Michael Marshall has remarked, 'When the worship is ended the service begins'. We encounter Jesus in word, sacrament and in each other in order that we might encounter him in the world and that the world might encounter him in us. We are sent out to participate in God's mission of love.

The word 'mass'—the popular Catholic term for the eucharist—deserves wider currency. It comes from the final injunction in the eucharist to 'go out'. The word 'mission' has the same root. Both, therefore, refer to God's sending. It is wise to keep this in mind as we turn to look at some specific issues relating this appreciation of the eucharist as parable and encounter to the ways in which we celebrate the eucharist in contemporary culture and, in particular, with children and young people. The eucharist makes us into a eucharistic people: we are re-membered by our celebration.

CLOTHING THE EUCHARIST IN CONTEMPORARY CULTURE

I have used the word 'liturgy' quite a few times in this chapter without properly explaining what it means. It is a crucial word for understanding how we celebrate the eucharist. It has taken on the meaning of 'words on a page' and is therefore often used to refer to the books containing set prayers and set orders of service, but the literal meaning is much more interesting: it is 'the work of the people'. We need to reconnect with this understanding of worship as a participatory drama rather than spectator event.

A cursory look at the traditional design of church buildings aptly illustrates our malaise. They speak of worship as something to be observed. Our problems are, quite literally, set in stone. The action is located at one raised and partitioned end of the building, being performed by the professionals, and everyone else is in the stalls (though, in the upside-down world of the Church, the best seats are at the back!) More progressive churches, with music groups and the like, have not changed the basic dynamic; they have just put a few more people on the stage. Incidentally, I do not intend to promulgate the dangerous Western heresy that you can only participate by being active— there is nothing worse than going to the theatre to watch a play and discovering to your horror as the curtain rises that you are part of the drama. However, I do want to redress the balance, to move away a little from thinking about liturgy as text and more towards thinking about liturgy as drama (parable and encounter). There is an irony here that in the Church of England, at the very moment of this rediscovery, we are blessed with a liturgical commission who are brilliant with words, when what we need are actions—they *do* speak much louder.

There are glorious examples of this new emphasis on liturgy

as the work of the people in the worship of many churches, where, by a reordering of their lives the people are discovering what it means to be a community of faith. I have the privilege of worshipping in one such church, St Thomas', Huddersfield. The reordering of the building and the liturgy express in ritual and movement a lot of what I have been saying about parable and encounter as the fusion of the key elements of eucharistic celebration.

On some occasions the whole assembly kisses the altar at the beginning of the eucharist. The worship space is divided so as to create movement between the place where we break open the word and the place we break open the bread. The priest sits in the body of the church with the congregation. Those who serve or read also emerge from the congregation to perform their ministry and then return. As many people as possible have jobs to do. There is a real sense of the community worshipping together. The focus of our attention is the story, symbolized by our gathering around the word of God; and sacramental encounter, symbolized by our gathering around the altar. What is created is community; an inspiring and nourishing celebration of the paschal mystery. We become an Easter people.

Another different, but equally challenging, example of this reworking of liturgy comes from those involved with what is unhelpfully known as 'alternative worship'. These are people seeking to reclaim liturgy as the work of the people by devising new acts of worship and new uses of ritual and symbol to reclothe Christian truth and Christian experience, often using contemporary forms such as video, and combining a heady brew of old and new.

The culture we live in is increasingly uneasy with the linear patters of some written communication. We usually receive information in a kaleidoscopic variety of dramatic, visual and sensual forms. This ought to inform the whole way the Church worships, but it is particularly relevant to the eucharist. This is an act of worship that is essentially visual and dramatic, not words on a page but a participatory drama in which the people of God gather around the table of the Lord to re-enact, celebrate and experience the paschal victory of Christ. At the heart of the eucharist are stories—which can be explored in so many ways other than simply by reading—and action—not just the words Jesus spoke but what he did with the bread and the wine.

Yet, as observed earlier, in many Christian communities today the eucharist is not understood. It is celebrated less frequently, and even then is often tagged on the end of a service focusing on the word of God. Moreover, it is thought 'difficult' for those outside, or on the edge of, the Christian community. Actually, instead, the eucharist could be our greatest asset. It has an objectivity that points us beyond the gifts and personality of the individuals leading the worship and can engage us at so many different levels of our being.

We need to reclothe the eucharist. We need to rediscover the potency of drama, ritual, symbol and action. Our first consideration must be more than the words we use; it must be the very space we occupy. We must think more creatively about the way we use our buildings, the way we arrange our chairs, the music we use, the images we project and the rituals we enact. Are they participatory drama? Do they engage and inspire? Are they telling the story in an involving way? Do they lead to encounter? When we do this, then the eucharist can become again our central act of worship, not just something we must continue because it's there in the Bible and we could hardly ditch it, but a life-changing, life-sustaining encounter.

This does not necessarily mean feverish activity, nor endless re-invention. Much of it is about creating space and simplicity in our worship. The basic story of the celebration needs to unfold clearly, the people of God gathered to hear the story of

God. We are part of that story so we should not be separated as if the story were separate from our lives. The word of God needs to take root in the midst of the assembly. All need an opportunity to read and hear. All need ways of bringing their own experiences and insights to bear. The word of God needs to be broken open. Sometimes this will mean exposition and proclamation, sometimes it will mean breaking into small groups to look at the scriptures together. (Why do we consider it appropriate to separate the children and let them explore the relevance of the word of God to their lives in all sorts of inter-active and stimulating ways, but the rest of us are supposed to get by on the same diet of readings and sermons week in week out?)

The main foci of the celebration—the encounter with Jesus in scripture, sacrament and each other—needs to be high-lighted with simple but challenging ritual. Our worship spaces need to be emptied of clutter. We need to see and have clearly defined the place for God's word, the place where God's holy people meet and the table where we share communion. Some-times it will be good for the places of the word and the sacra-ment to be separate, so we can move from one to another, just as it is good to have a separate place for coffee and fellowship after the celebration. We need to employ modern media to help tell the story and accentuate the encounter—projected images to focus our attention, music to still and inspire, video to instruct and describe. We need to rediscover and have fresh confidence in the old media. Lights and incense, drama and dance speak powerfully into the deep and secret places of our being. This is where God will find us. This is where most of us are crying out for love and affirmation. We live in an age where people, especially the young, are searching for spiritual truth. Let us make our churches spiritual places, and in worship let us enable head and heart and hands to sing in harmony.

This is the way to approach the eucharist. Not just with our head, but with our whole being. Not just with a book, but with a whole people.

CELEBRATING THE EUCHARIST

WITH CHILDREN

In my experience, children readily understand and appreciate the mystery of the eucharist. The three encounters with Jesus —in word, sacrament and one another—provide the basic pattern for the celebration.

In preparing to celebrate the eucharist with children, we might say that the eucharist is a way of meeting Jesus (encounter) and a way of joining in and understanding the story of his love (parable). We might say something like this: 'We cannot hear Jesus speaking to us today like people could when he was alive on earth, but we can hear him speak when we read the Bible. We cannot feel him holding us or blessing us, but we can feel his love in other people. We cannot experience him feeding us like he fed the five thousand or shared supper with his friends, but he does feed us when we share bread and wine as he asked.'

The celebration of the eucharist can then be presented to the children as a party. All parties mark special occasions. The special occasions the eucharist marks are the life, death and resurrection of Jesus. It is a thank you party to God for Jesus, and in the party Jesus speaks to us, loves and feeds us. The party is held in his honour, but he is also the special guest coming to us in the three ways described above.

We are then sent back to our homes, our community, our classrooms to live our lives like Jesus. We try to speak and act like him. We try to listen and love like him. We try to feed others and share like him. We have received a blessing; we try to be a blessing to others.

We can also show that the pattern of the eucharist is breaking and sharing. We open the Bible to find out how God loves us, and how we should live our lives. We open ourselves to love one another, to build a better world. We break open the bread to share with one another.

In an actual celebration of the eucharist these 'meetings' with Jesus flow through the celebration. If the theme of the service is, for instance, journeys, then in scripture we might pick one of the great stories of a journey, such as the Exodus, and explore it in drama, dance, written and art work. With one another we might explore what it means to be together on a journey. In sharing bread and wine we might describe these as our rations for the journey of life and think about what other basic things we need to take with us. In being sent out into the world we might think about how we are called to be living signposts to Jesus.

There is, of course, the question of celebrating the eucharist with children when they are often excluded from receiving communion itself. The regulations for this are different in many denominations, and in the Church of England this is a changing situation. It is now possible for children to be admitted to the eucharist before confirmation and this practice is slowly taking root. It is my strong view that children who attend church ought to be able to receive communion. As baptized members of the body of Christ we should all be eligible to share at Christ's table.

However, even if children are not receiving communion, it is good to emphasize the totality of the service—meeting and receiving Jesus in different ways. Children can be involved in the drama of the eucharist by helping to bake the bread beforehand, acting out the readings, writing the prayers, constructing the altar, making vestments and banners and preparing and leading the music. This will all help to make the worship their own and help them look forward to the time when they can receive communion rather than feel excluded from it, as they may well feel otherwise. The worship also needs to be arranged so that everyone receives a blessing. This can be presented as the way Jesus blesses children today. There are several gospel stories of Jesus blessing children and a blessing can easily be linked to the blessing of the eucharist.

We should also take note that some children (and indeed some adults!) are concerned about the body and blood language used when speaking about the consecrated bread and wine. As we have already noted, it is the risen life of Jesus that is communicated to us in the bread and wine. God takes ordinary things and gives them a new value. This is the pattern throughout the Christian faith.

For children, we can say that God 'uses' the bread and wine to feed us with the life of Jesus. Just as Jesus fed his friends on earth, so he feeds us today. We can also develop the idea of things being special and different. Just as we decorate a cake with candles and it becomes a birthday cake, God adorns the bread and wine to celebrate Jesus—the bread becomes special or holy bread.

We can also develop the analogy of money referred to earlier. A piece of paper is printed with a certain design and it becomes a ten-pound note. It is still a piece of paper, but now it is a special piece of paper with a new value. Similarly, God gives the bread of the eucharist a new value.

These are all ideas that children can enter into. If they are communicated in the flow of a service in which they have creative participation, then this will lead to an experience of the Christian faith that is, for them, a living parable and a life-giving encounter. This is what the eucharist is all about. Matter matters. Bread becomes a vehicle for communicating the life of Jesus. Human beings become temples for the Holy Spirit. Ordinary surroundings become sacred and holy.

CELEBRATING THE EUCHARIST
WITH YOUNG PEOPLE

Everything that has been said for children is doubly true for teenagers. More than any other group of people, they are open to the drama and delight of eucharistic worship when it focuses on parable and encounter. Thus it has been one of the great joys of my ministry to celebrate the eucharist with young people on all sorts of weird and wonderful occasions. By the side of the road on walking pilgrimages, using an icebox for an altar and a tin cup for a chalice; in a church hall; on a windswept Yorkshire moor at dawn; with still tenderness and riveting drama when the young people themselves organized the whole shape of the liturgy, and, although the eucharist itself lasted three or four times longer than normal, it seemed in its unfolding dramatization of God's love and invitation a single moment of eternity. Every one of these celebrations has been an annunciation— God has come to me, formed Jesus within me and shown me more of what it means to be his Church.

None of this means that we should not observe the basic shape of the eucharist that has been passed to us from the very earliest days of the Church; nor the important regulations about the eucharist that each denomination has established. For instance, in all the major denominations, only an ordained minister can consecrate the bread and wine. This is important as it reminds us that there is only one eucharist—the eternal offering of the Son to the Father in which we participate—and the priest, as a representative of Christ to the people and the people to Christ, preserves and proclaims the unity of God's Church. What I wish to emphasize here, however, is that we are a priestly people. So, once we have understood the basic shape of the eucharist and explored the particular ways in which Jesus is encountered, there is room for much creativity. The role of the ordained minister is to preside—to oversee the work of the people as they make celebrations of the eucharist together.

CONCLUSION

'To celebrate' means to make famous, to publish the praises. This is what we do in the eucharist—we make famous and publish the praises of the one whose story brings life and in whose story we find the meaning of our lives.

When Jesus taught about the kingdom of God, he usually spoke in parables. They are not always easy to understand. Likewise, sometimes the eucharist is not easy to understand, and it is all too easy to take it for granted. Sometimes the parables of Jesus are pithy riddles, sometimes they are elaborate stories. In turn, they infuriate, encourage, rebuke and inspire. Using parallels from ordinary life, Jesus likens the reign of God to a coming harvest, leavening dough, hidden treasure and priceless jewels. Precise meaning, however, can be elusive.

There is a depth and range in Jesus' storytelling that means we will come back to his sayings again and again, finding new insights that speak to new experiences. Like a great work of art, it is insufficient to simply ask 'What does it mean?' In order to understand the meaning, you need to live inside the story. Thus we discover that the kingdom of God is not a designated region, nor citizenship measured by adherence to a code, but that the boundaries of God's kingdom run through human hearts, and that this is one kingdom that does not have a king to whom we must fearfully submit, but a father who pours out his love to his wayward children.

Jesus' words and actions at the last supper are like an acted parable. They speak of God's reign and his love. Like all the parables there are levels of meaning to be uncovered. The puzzling intrigue of Jesus' words draws us closer not to a body of teaching that we admire and wish to follow, but to a teacher who embodies all that he proclaims.

The only way to understand the eucharist is to celebrate it. The way of celebrating the eucharist that will take us beyond a dry recitation of text and an empty observation of dated ceremonial is to reclothe the eucharist as parable and encounter. Thus we, the people of God, tell the story of God's love using our own insights, experiences and gifts; and as we do so we meet Jesus, present in our midst, inviting us to his table.

3

THE EUCHARIST
AND THE
POST-MODERN
WORLD

Graham Cray

WHAT'S SO SPECIAL
ABOUT THE EUCHARIST?

The eucharist lies at the heart of Christian life. It is the act of worship in which the central core of the biblical gospel is retold and re-enacted, the focal point of Christian worship. If any part of traditional Christian practice is relevant to the post-modern era it must be the eucharist, or at least the gospel that the eucharist sums up.

However, as our culture continues to take on both a post-modern shape and post-modern perspectives, we have to admit that there is nothing about the eucharist or any other Christian practice that excludes it from a post-modern critique. Full-blown deconstructivist post-modernism is irreconcilable with biblical Christian faith. So this is a serious matter.

Post-modernity is the sociological term for the emerging shape of Western societies at the close of the twentieth century.

It is also the name for the perspectives on the nature of truth that are currently fashionable in many academic circles. The two terms reinforce one another. As we seem to be entering a new cultural era, so we need new perspectives on truth in order to make sense of it. As we experience life in new ways, some fashionable claims about truth seem self-evident. For many people who have never heard of post-modernism and who will never use the term, its claims just seem to be common sense. Post-modernity makes post-modernism seem plausible.

Post-modern thinking is that it is no longer possible to believe in 'grand narratives', meaning stories that claim to be universally true or the key to all other truths. But every eucharistic prayer conveys a grand narrative! 'Christ has died, Christ is risen, Christ will come again' relates the whole of history to what Jesus Christ has done, is now and will be. Eucharistic prayers usually rehearse the purpose and actions of God from creation to the hope of a new creation. In the form of a prayer of thanksgiving they convey an all-inclusive claim about the nature and purpose of the world. Post-modern thinking sees all such truth claims as illegitimate plays for power. Claiming that the gospel is true and that other people should accept it and reorder their lives around it because of its truth, is, to a post-modernist, an illegitimate attempt at control, an ideological power play. Applying this to the eucharist, liturgists speak of the 'deep structures' of the major acts of Christian worship.[1] From the perspective of post-modern suspicion, all such liturgy would be seen as a controlling subtext, a spiritually cloaked form of oppression.

Another claim of post-modern philosophy relates to the slipperiness or indeterminacy of language. Jacques Derrida claims that 'there is nothing outside the text'[2] and that a text (liturgical or otherwise) is no more than 'a fabric of traces referring endlessly to something other than itself, to other differential traces'.[3] Were this to be so, then liturgical texts and eucharistic prayers, with their long histories of development, would neither contain nor convey the relatively fixed meanings that Christians claim for them. There would then be little to restrain the 'free play of meaning'.

Is liturgy, then, a self-deceiving 'act of mastery' by Christians who, in fact, constructed whatever they cared to believe in, while convincing themselves that they were responding to truths that had been revealed to them?

Post-modern society has moved from a realist understanding of truth—the belief that truth exists whether we believe it or not—to a constructivist view—that 'truths' are things we invent or choose to believe in order to get by. Our consumer culture then provides the criteria for the choice or construction of truths that suit us.

> When the only criteria left for choosing... are learned in the marketplace, the truth appears as a commodity. We hear that people 'buy into' a belief or that, rather than rejecting a dogma as false; they 'cannot buy' this or that viewpoint.[4]

The models for assembling DIY truths are drawn from the pick and mix sweet counter or the digital sampler (using a fragment of an existing record as a component in the creation of a new one). One post-modern philosopher may have called this sort of eclecticism 'the degree zero of contemporary general culture',[5] but it is increasingly the way in which Western people create makeshift worldviews.

The implication for the eucharist, and its grand story of God's purposes made manifest in Christ, is that it is reduced to one source among many. It is then a repository from which people can withdraw anything they like, from a cross or crucifix to be used as a fashion object, to a claim to have encountered Jesus as a complement to their experience of Krishna or a New Age spiritual guide. Douglas Coupland, the author of *Generation X*, calls this 'Me-ism. A search by an individual in the absence of training in traditional religious tenets to formulate a personally tailored religion by himself'.[6]

Another element of post-modernism invites its audience to 'enjoy the surface' of life's experiences because there is nothing beneath the surface. In other words, nothing is sacramental, nothing points beyond itself to anything else. Each experience is what it is or does to you, there is nothing beyond. From this perspective the eucharist may give a sense of awe or of the ancient or even community, but it can never be more than a sense, a vibe. Any such experience is understood as a feeling to be fleetingly enjoyed, it could never be more. So, from this perspective, while the eucharist gives you a buzz, go for it. When it doesn't and the 'been there, done that, so this place has no more to offer' feeling comes over you, then move on to something stranger.

Closely linked to this is the post-modern emphasis on the significance of the present moment. Not 'the sacrament of the present moment',[7] as understood in some spiritual writing, but the present moment because the present is all there is to be sure of. Life is understood as a perpetual present or, rather, a series of perpetual presents—a perpetual sequence of living for the moment. From this point of view, 'the goal of life' is 'an endless pursuit of new experiences, values and vocabularies'.[8] Whatever feels good *is* good. Such a view robs the eucharist of its narrative structure, its capacity to give meaning to our lives through a telling of God's story as it affects past, present and future. Rather than offering hope for the future, it would be seen as merely the latest thing to move on from.

The centrepiece of post-modernity is consumerism. The consumer culture is characterized by obsolescence and is founded on a perpetually broken promise. In the consumer culture, everything is made to be bought but nothing is made to last. 'A throw away society meant more than just throwing away produced goods, but also being able to throw away values, lifestyles, stable relationships... and received ways of doing and being.'[9] This has a corrosive impact on any sense of meaning or direction in life. 'The transitoriness of things makes it difficult to preserve any sense of historical continuity.'[10] The perpetually broken promise is that of a happiness always but elusively available in the next purchase. In a culture built on obsolescence 'consumerism promises something it can't deliver'.[11]

If the post-modern experience and interpretation of the world is accurate, then the eucharist has no contemporary defence. It will not disappear, it will simply become the victim of what each one chooses to make of it or with it. The sign of God's eternal promise in Christ will become just another part of a culture of broken promises.

A THREE-DIMENSIONAL RITE FOR A ONE-DIMENSIONAL CULTURE

THE PROMISE OF THE EUCHARIST IN A POST-MODERN AGE

If instead we consider the eucharist on its own, traditional terms, it appears to offer everything that post-modern society lacks. The consumer focus on the perpetual present is the result of two dislocations. First, Western peoples have largely lost their sense of being rooted in the past. The thinking of the Enlightenment brought about a drastic change in the everyday meaning of the word 'revolution'. It lost the sense of 'here we go around again' and, courtesy of the French and Industrial Revolutions, came to mean a radical discontinuity from the insights, authority and experience of any previous era. At the core of these new developments was a 'rejection of the past as a source of inspira-

tion or example'.[12] Any sense of history is then replaced by a
heritage industry in which we demonstrate our technical clever-
ness by recreating the past, so that tourists can experience its
strangeness. This is part of the culture of the spectacle and of
the voyeur.[13] In future, some people may 'sample' an occasional
eucharist on precisely this basis. Some do so already when they
visit a cathedral as a tourist rather than a pilgrim, and make an
on-the-spot decision to stay on for a service. We have become a
rootless society. Indeed, this has been the case for most of the
post-Enlightenment era, but it did not seem to involve any element of loss while science and technology appeared to offer an
ever-improving future. Western belief in progress, of a better
world on the way, more than compensated for the loss of roots.

The second dislocation is that we now live in an age deeply
uncertain about the future, and highly aware of the double-
edged nature of science and technology. 'Living in the modern
world is more like being aboard a careering juggernaut rather
than being in a carefully controlled and well-driven motor
car.'[14] This radical questioning about the future has led to an
overemphasis on the present. We live for now because now is
all we can be sure of. Furthermore, having gambled all on our
own scientific and technological brilliance, we have nothing else
to look to. As Jean Baudrillard has written:

> Cultures stranger than ours live in prostration (before the heavens,
> before destiny); we live in consternation (at the absence of destiny).
> Nothing can come from anywhere except from us. This is, in a way,
> the most absolute misfortune.[15]

It would indeed be the most absolute misfortune if it were true!
However, in each eucharist (each giving of thanks for what God
has done in Christ) the Church proclaims an alternative perspective. This call to praise comes from the maker of us all, for
'praise is... the ultimate vocation of the human community;
indeed of all creation'.[16]

When we give thanks (Greek *eucharisto*) we are responding to our maker, who exists beyond our everyday reality, but stepped into it in Jesus Christ. In the face of post-modern despair, Christian theology, Christian mission and Christian liturgy proclaim 'we are not alone, something (someone) does come from somewhere other than us'.

Post-modern society, as we have seen, has a one-dimensional perspective. It needs a three-dimensional gospel. Christian worship, and especially the eucharist, links past, present and future. 'It is the appointed place at which the past, present and future of God's dealings with man in Christ come to clear, concrete and climactic expression.'[17] In the eucharist we are celebrating the Lord's death in the past, but we do so in his risen presence and in anticipation of his return.

Christians claim that what God has done in Christ restores both a rootedness in the past and a hope for the future. Both are necessary for any sense of meaning in life beyond the here and now. 'In order to have a sense of who we are, we have to have a notion of how we have become, and of where we are going.'[18] Tradition is not a term taken seriously by those raised to seek continually after the latest fashionable experience, but 'to live in tradition is about living an authentic life in which our present is given coherence from our past and hope from our future'.[19]

Post-modern society is also marked by fragmentation. Its primary coherence is provided by consumerism, but 'consumer society is individualistic by definition'.[20] Both social theorists and popular artists point out the fragmented nature of our culture. Damon Albarn of Blur has spoken of 'how fragmented the world is... Never have people thought so hard about their lives and come to such indecision, or felt further apart'.[21] Similarly, sociologist Zygmunt Bauman claims:

> In a cacophony of moral voices, none of which is likely to silence the others, the individuals are thrown back on their own subjectivity as the only ultimate ethical authority... There are no obvious

social agencies that may guide the choice between indifference and solidarity.[22]

The eucharist, however, affirms the possibility of human reconciliation by means of reconciliation with God. The bread that is shared points not only to the death of Christ, which restores our relationship with God, but also to the body that is his Church. It thus reaffirms the hope of community, of lasting relationships.

Many Western people have lost any sense of the love of God, and certainly of a God who acts in love towards them personally. Some show this in their quest for some form of spirituality—for no one searches for what they already have. Others maintain belief in a God who is too distant to matter—he doesn't make any difference. Sociologist Grace Davie reports a social survey interview as follows:

'Do you believe in God?'

'Yes.'

'Do you believe in a God who can change the course of events on earth?'

'No, just the ordinary one.'[23]

The Christian faith proclaims, and its eucharist affirms, the personal, relational love of God for all people—what one philosopher called 'a divine affirmation of the human, more total than humans can ever attain unaided'.[24]

IS THERE ANYTHING BENEATH

THE SURFACE?

Is this Christian claim a construction? Is the traditional interpretation the inevitable meaning of the eucharist—in which case Christians have a profound contribution to make to our contemporary culture—or is it the meaning Christians choose to believe to help themselves get by in a confused and confusing age? The critical question is this, is there anything beneath the eucharistic surface? Is the eucharist a rite that is malleable to any interpretation or does it involve a 'real' encounter with God?

> *Worship can have the power to convert or (and alas, this is more frequent) to repel. It is not just that the conduct of worship can be amazingly incompetent; it is that people have a very real sense of whether what is being offered is the genuine article or not.*[25]

If, as some Christians imply, the eucharist is merely a symbolic visual aid, a supplement to the sermon, then it has no way of resisting the attacks of post-modern relativism. It will become whatever different groups try to make of it. However, if 'beneath the surface' is a life-changing encounter with a living God, then a whole new factor is involved. In this case, an Anglo- or Roman Catholic theology is not required in order to believe in the reality of an encounter with God in the eucharist. Paul warns the Corinthians of the danger of eating and drinking 'judgment against themselves' and of being 'answerable for the body and blood of the Lord'. He even says that eating and drinking in an unworthy manner has resulted in the sickness, weakness or even death of some (1 Corinthians 11:27–32)! In which case, there is certainly something beneath the surface. Reformed theologian Alan Torrance has written that 'worship may be described as an event—in which the kingdom of God is "in a manner" actually and freely present—and not merely future'.[26]

An event in which the kingdom of God is actually present is a far cry from a constructivist view, for constructivism changes nothing beyond the mindset of the constructor. In Iain Banks' novel *A Song of Stone*, his main character says:

All is construction in the end... But we are the naming beast, the animal that thinks with language, and all above us is called what we choose, for lack of better terms, and everything we name means—as far as we are concerned—just what we want it to connote. There is a reciprocity of insult for our name-calling here; for our fine defining words tame nothing in the end, and should we ever fall victim to the unseen grammar of life, we must brave the elements and suffer their indifference, fully requited in return.[27]

The eucharist, though, offers a positive alternative to the 'naming beast', one in which eternal reality bites back. We are indeed 'naming' creatures (Genesis 2:19), but our authority to name comes with a responsible relationship with God as his stewards. The eucharist offers an encounter with this living God in a number of ways.

First of all, like all other expressions of worship, it is a gift received from God, before it is an activity engaged in by Christians. 'Worship is a gift of grace which is realized vicariously in Christ and which is received and participated in by the Spirit' and 'It is precisely the theological insight that God's grace actually includes the provision of the very response demanded that distinguishes Christian worship from religious ritual.'[28] As an expression of his grace, God frees us to worship. 'The experience of the transcendent freedom of God who chooses to come into our midst and to create in us the freedom to respond to him is the essence of worship.'[29] Before any experience of God in worship, God has acted to make worship possible. In worship he comes towards us before we come towards him. This is why the deepest human instinct is to worship.

Christian worship is to be 'in the Spirit' and it is the presence of the Holy Spirit that makes worship an actual encounter with God. Without this, the eucharist is little more than an insecure repetition, telling ourselves a story over and over that we are trying to believe. Paul, on the other hand, says it is 'a participation... in the blood and body of Christ' (1 Corinthians 10:16, NIV). This participation is made possible by the Spirit. John Calvin was the Reformation theologian with the clearest emphasis on the role of the Spirit in the sacraments. Brian Gerrish summarizes Calvin's emphasis in this way: 'The sacraments are strictly the Spirit's means or instruments: where the Spirit is absent, the sacraments achieve no more than the sun shining on blind eyes or a voice sounding in deaf ears.'[30] In the eucharist, then, there is an actual encounter with Christ by the Spirit.

> *The eucharistic gift is a real participation in the glorified life of Christ which he lives in the presence of the Father... Our participation in the ascended Christ in the eucharist is made possible by the work of the Spirit.* [31]

The encounter with Christ in the eucharist may be a gift available through grace, but it is not inevitable. We never have an encounter with God forced on us. Every initiative God takes towards us is for the sake of a relationship. If Christ is truly present in his Spirit (irrespective of the theological arguments about the locality of his presence), he is, as ever, to be met through faith. Gerrish again summarizes Calvin's teaching: 'The eucharistic gift benefits those only who respond with the faith that the proclamation itself generates.'[32] In other words, just to be present is not automatically to encounter Christ. The gospel is proclaimed in eucharistic liturgy, both in the ministry of the word and in the prayer of thanksgiving. As ever, the gospel is proclaimed to awaken faith. As ever, it can also be rejected. There is either grace or judgment to be met here.

> *As the Church gathers around the Lord's table in remembrance of him, believing that... this is truly the Lord's supper, in which bread and wine are a 'participation in the body and blood of Christ', we are confronted with the... reality of Christ's gift of himself which we may either welcome by faith or reject to our judgment.* [33]

If the gospel is true, Christ is objectively present to be encountered by faith whenever Christians celebrate the eucharist in fulfilment of his command. There is not some*thing* but some-*one* beneath the surface of eucharistic worship. However, the encounter with him can be for the worse as well as for better.

When met by faith, this gospel encounter has a twin focus. From the past, we receive the renewal and reassurance of the forgiveness of sins that resulted from the work of the cross. There is no repetition of Christ's once-for-all work in eucharistic worship (Hebrews 9:26), but there is a repetition of an account of that work so that, once more, we can receive and be renewed by it through faith: 'In gratitude the past is repeated in such a way that it is fruitful in a new way for the present and the future.'[34] As forgiven people, we also receive an anticipation of the future, the personal presence and empowering of the Holy Spirit. This is the power of the resurrection to strengthen us for a lifestyle shaped by the cross (Philippians 3:10). Each of these gifts—the renewal of forgiveness and the empowering for discipleship—is rooted in the cross and ministered to us by the ascended Christ through his Spirit:

Just as in the anamnesis (remembrance) of his death, the power of his past is present with us, so in the anticipation of his parousia (return) the power of his future is also present and active among us.[35]

Liturgy provides the secure context for this risky, life-changing encounter with the risen Christ.

EVANGELISM OR EDIFICATION?

The eucharist has great power and significance for the post-modern era, but is it a direct or an indirect resource for the

Church's mission. Who or what is it for? Is it to make Christians more like Christ or is it to attract outsiders? Is it, as John Wesley claimed, a converting ordinance?

In one sense there is no question to answer. Self-evidently the eucharist is the sacrament of our continuing relationship with Christ, just as baptism marks its beginning. 'We may identify the eucharist as the dominically appointed context both for the renewal of our identification with Christ's death and for the intensification of our participation in his life'.[36] Alan Kreider has pointed out that the significance of worship for the mission of the early Church was not that it was attractive to outsiders, but that it helped to shape Christlike lives in the world, and these lives were profoundly attractive:

> Worship, to which pagans were denied admission, was all important in the spread of the Church. It was important not because it was attractive, but because its rites and practices... made differences in the lives and communities of the worshippers. It performed the function of re-forming those pagans who joined the Church into Christians, into distinctive people who lived in a way that was recognizably in the tradition of Jesus Christ.[37]

An act of worship made too accessible to post-modern consumers may be at the cost of the very elements that are central to the building up of Christians. It may also, in the post-modern era, lack the very elements that would most profoundly challenge, and ultimately attract, 'seekers'. As Bryan Spinks has said, 'If anything, the problem is to guard against the modern liturgies being just a religious gloss on a developing Western culture.'[38] 'Seeker-friendly' worship is important, but it must be authentic Christian worship. First, and above all, worship is for God (Ephesians 5:19–20), a gift received and given back in gratitude. If either edification or evangelism usurp the God-directed focus of worship, it ceases to be Christian worship. Only then, as an overflow of grace, is worship a gift of God that will build up the Church (1 Corinthians 14:26), in particular strengthening it for an ethical life and witness in society. Robin Gill has pointed out the moral impact of Christian worship: 'Within worship moral values take on a more demanding and insistent shape than they do outside worship: they change the very way we see the world.'[39] Finally, as part of its ecology, worship has an overflow for the non-believer, who discovers that 'God is really among you' (1 Corinthians 14:24–25).

Daniel Hardy and David Ford have written of 'evangelism as the horizontal dimension of praise—the content of praise repeated and explained to others so that they can join the community of praise'.[40] This has a particularly powerful application in the post-modern world, which is a world full of signs in which nothing is truly sacramental. Nothing is understood as pointing to anything of significance beyond itself. In practice, the majority of contemporary icons point to something less than themselves, as they are used to convey the empty promises of consumerism. Andrew Walker has pointed out the significance of liturgy in this context:

> In this world where icons proliferate but are profane; where texts swarm everywhere but have lost their sting; where images dominate our senses but mirror each other, liturgy is a beacon to show the way out. People may be alienated by outdated traditions, but in a post-modern world liturgy is new and mysterious, numinous and beckoning. To come to the liturgy is to penetrate sameness, to discover for the first time transcendence and otherness; to experience words and images, signs and symbols that have a reference point beyond themselves.[41]

THE PROOF IS IN THE EATING

How may the open-minded unbeliever know that this ritual with bread, wine and the retelling of Christ's story is a place of

God's presence and actually points to the truth about God and all of human life?

It is increasingly likely that enquirers about the Christian message will be present in services of worship before any final commitment to faith. This is not because of a 'celebration evangelism' approach, but because evangelism in this post-modern context is increasingly being understood as a process. We have reinvented the catechumen in Alpha, Emmaus and so on. Post-modern people know so little about the Christian faith that evangelism takes longer and starts further back than in the past. It involves exposing them to the reality of the Christian life, not just teaching them Christian beliefs. It often involves tentative membership of the Christian community ahead of permanent commitment; belonging before believing. This places worship on the frontline of mission.

For such enquirers, there must be some sense of encounter, some tangible sense of awe that is the direct consequence of the truth of the gospel and the presence of the Spirit. Post-modern people crave experience. They need to have it themselves or see it in others. Worship needs to create a hunger for God in those who do not yet know him, just as it satisfies and yet deepens that hunger in believers. There is the danger that post-modern people seek experience for its own sake, that they become no more than sensation gatherers, but an experienceless Christianity is not New Testament Christianity and will never commend the faith. Churchmanship may be high or low; the worship may be liturgical or more spontaneous, the focus may be on the word or the Spirit, but there is no substitute for encountering the presence of the living God.

Once again, an overemphasis on accessibility may be unwise: *Christianity's talent for shooting itself in the foot is nowhere better displayed than in its recent drive to demystify itself. After all, who goes into a church to get reasonable? Mystery is precisely what used to draw the crowds; no wonder gates are down.*[42]

One way or another, the experience that 'God is among you' or 'you people have something' or some similar sense of awareness of the transcendent is the essential starting point.

There must be encounter with God, but experience alone is not enough to confront a post-modern worldview. Conscious encounter with the God of love needs to be supported by the evidence of love as the fruit of the Spirit. Post-modernity is full of experiences but bereft of reconciliation and lasting relationships. People are thirsty for a community of love.

The dance music scene is one of the more substantial recent developments that has raised and dashed people's hopes of a safe community. The band Faithless sings of a club night in this way: 'This is my church. This is where I heal my hurt. For tonight God is a DJ'.[43] Sadly, a night at a club falls a long way short of a community of reconciled and committed relationships. Furthermore, the club scene is commercially driven and also, substantially, a drug scene. Richard Benson, editor of the style magazine *The Face*, wrote, 'It sometimes seems that, sadly, alongside only wars and nostalgia an escapist class A drug is the only thing that currently creates a sense of communal experience across society's fault lines.'[44] An ardent advocate of the dance culture (a culture in which I also see much good) shares similar concerns:

> I worry sometimes whether recreational drug use is any kind of adequate basis for a culture, let alone a counter-culture. Is rave simply about the dissipation of utopian energies into the void, or does the idealism it catalyses spill over into and transform ordinary life? ... Learning to 'lose your self' can be an enlightenment, but it can also be strangely selfish: a greed for intense, ravishing experiences.[45]

The critical question, which is to be asked also of the eucharist, is do its effects spill over into and transform ordinary life? David le Jars in *The Big Issue* told of an unplanned attendance at a rite—a eucharist in the chapel of a retreat centre, which he had visited simply as a tourist. What struck him most was the sharing of peace:

> *I can't escape the fact that the service was one of the most spiritually liberating experiences I've ever had. It wasn't because of the words, or the actions or the dogma. It was, I think, because of the underlying assumption of community. The sense that, in this fragmented society of ours, where the spiritual is perpetually sidelined in favour of the material; where loving thy neighbour is something you do when the neighbour's husband is out at work; it's actually OK to be soulful.*[46]

If the sharing of peace demonstrates deeply committed relationship and a hospitable Church culture, it is remarkable evidence for the fruitfulness of the gospel and its capacity to grow a community of love. If it is no more than a rather embarrassing ritual, giving clear evidence that these people do not really know or care for one another, who would want to become a Christian anyway?

Worship should be an embodied sign of that future time when God will bring about his final reconciliation, the reconciliation which Christ died to establish (Colossians 1:20). This is, perhaps, easier to see in a racist or manifestly oppressive situation, as described by Desmond Tutu when he was Dean of Johannesburg:

> *As I have knelt in the Dean's stall at the superb 9.30 high mass, with incense, bells and everything, watching a multiracial crowd file up to the altar rails to be communicated, the one bread and one cup given by a mixed team of clergy and lay ministers with a multiracial choir, servers and sidemen—all this in apartheid-mad South Africa—then tears of joy sometimes streamed down my cheeks, tears of joy that it could be indeed that Jesus Christ had broken down the wall of partition, that here were the first fruits of the eschatological community right in front of my eyes.*[47]

However, the same reconciliation needs to be demonstrated in fragmented, late twentieth-century consumer societies, with their desperate need for authentic community. It is the double meaning of 'the body of Christ' in the eucharist that gives it its evangelistic potential.

Ultimately, if the eucharist is to have an evangelistic surplus, then it must act as a call to obedience. Not just initial obedience by conversion to Christ, but also ongoing obedience by exhibiting Christlike discipleship in the world. David Ford has pointed out the imperatives that run through the New Testament accounts of the last supper.[48] The command is 'Do this in remembrance of me.' On this side of the resurrection it is impossible to take communion without facing the call to obey Christ. The test of any professed obedience, whether expressed liturgically in the saying of the creed or more personally in a prayer of commitment, is the life that results in the everyday world. It is totally appropriate that the Church of England's eucharistic liturgy concludes with 'Send us out in the power of your Spirit to live and work to your praise and glory'. Whether eucharistic or not, 'worship makes strong demands upon us. It requires no less than we should go out into the world to love, serve and care'.[49]

THE EUCHARIST AND
THE QUESTION OF IDENTITY

The post-modern challenge to Christian belief has been presented in these pages as a challenge about the nature of faith. However, the post-modern dilemma is not finally about truth but, rather, about identity. The question is not what can we know or even how can we know? The question is who are we who struggle to know? Post-modern literature is full of questioning about identity and the nature of the self. As with issues of truth, post-modern thinking has proved better at deconstructing previous understandings of the self than it has at establishing new ones. We have clearly moved a long way from the Enlightenment's centred self—observing and controlling the world and its future. Instead, we have a de-centred self, knowing it is not anywhere near as free as Western culture once claimed.

> *The post-modern self knows what it is to be trapped by its own past decisions and placed in bondage to a situatedness which is not of its own choice. It knows the need to be released from external forces beyond its control, and to be delivered from the tyranny of corporate self-interests and competing power-interests.* [50]

This de-centred self is seen in two forms. Despite the disillusion with the Enlightenment's understanding of the self, there are optimistic and pessimistic post-moderns. The pessimists accept the loss of fixed identity, but grieve its consequences. The self is seen as fragmented,[51] 'shattered'. Identity and personal coherence become a problem. One survival strategy is that of addiction or of withdrawal into a narrowly defined life. The self 'contracts to a defensive core'.[52]

The optimists see identity as multichoice. We can be whoever we want to be, dependent on the circumstances. Consumer choice provides the key to identity: 'Lifestyle choice is increasingly important in the constitution of self-identity.'[53] At the heart of the multichoice approach is a search for identity, but a refusal to be tied down, to be answerable: 'The hub of post-modern life strategy is not identity building but avoidance of fixation'; 'Keep the options open.'[54] In Christian terms, this is a contemporary expression of sin, of our refusal to bow before our maker and be tied down to faithfulness in that relationship.

In practice, both the optimists and the pessimists are

extremely vulnerable to the pressure to fit in with other people's expectations. The move from modern to post-modern involves a move from being 'inner-centred' to being 'other-centred'—that is, shaped by our concern about what others think of us. The pessimists are anxious not to be seen or to make trouble. The optimists want to play the game of belonging, wherever they are. In either case, the model for identity is the chameleon. In both strategies the authentic, God-given self shrivels.

The Christian contribution to this debate asserts that we are relational selves, made in the image of a relational God. We are made to thrive, not shrink, in relationships. To be truly human is neither to withdraw nor to role play, but to interact and love out of a secure sense of personal identity and worth. For this to be possible, we must first be worshipping selves.[55] It is in response to God, who made us and entered his own creation to redeem and restore us, that we find our true selves. The human self thrives and undergoes moral transformation when it responds to God's call to worship.

> *Religious communities are... communities responding in worship to Another, not communities manufacturing and then maintaining values. Values for them are grounded in an attempt to understand external reality at its most profound level. In short, they are grounded in metaphysics.*[56]

'Morality is... intimately linked to worship.' The eucharist is the act of worship that sums up all our Creator Redeemer is and has done. It is here that the gospel is rehearsed again. It is here that Christian character is stretched in response to the transcendent God:

> *Repetition after repetition of hearing scripture and its interpretation, of repentance, of intercession and petition, of the kiss of peace, of communion, of praising and thanksgiving, all within a dramatic pattern that slowly becomes second nature: who can tell*

in advance what sort of self is being shaped year after year as these practices are woven thoughtfully with all the rest of life. [57]

It is here that some of the post-modern age will hear the call to believe and obey. 'For as often as you eat this bread and drink this cup, you proclaim the Lord's death until he comes' (1 Corinthians 11:26, NRSV).

4

BREAD AND WINE, BEER AND PIES

Mike Riddell

Inside the dance and music venue where Parallel Universe is meeting, it is dark. The floor of the vast cavern is populated by tables, around which groups of people are seated, some drinking. There may be just a hint on the nose of sweat and stale beer from last night's concert. Three huge screens dominate the visual landscape. On them there is a changing montage of video and slides, bearing dramatic scenery interspersed with the work of contemporary New Zealand artists. Music is playing, original work by local musicians. On the tables there are various kiwiana artefacts. This is Parallel Universe, at worship. The theme of the evening is 'Your Soul Needs A Lift: A celebration of kiwi culture'.

Suddenly the music drops. From various points around the floor, people emerge bearing trays. They are dressed in the waiters' uniform of white shirts and black waistcoats. Slowly they advance through the crowd, until they gather in a circle around a covered table in the centre of proceedings. They turn to face outwards—all eyes are on them. Then they look up, and all the eyes follow. There is a swelling of music, and lo and behold, descending from the extremely high ceiling are bottles of wine! Eight bottles of a very good Chardonnay, to be precise, coming down from on high. Each waiter receives one and proceeds to open it.

The cover is removed from the table to reveal a magnificent

pavlova—a national sweet composed mostly of meringue—decorated, of course, with kiwi fruit. This is ceremonially sliced, then the waiters begin to distribute the Chardonnay and pavlova among the gathered crowd. Communion is not mentioned. There is no prayer of consecration, nor words of institution, simply the serving, eating and drinking.

The Christians in the crowd look at each other. What was that? Was it the eucharist? Is it legitimate? The questions remain unanswered as the worship has already moved on to the reading of work by a New Zealand poet. Later, the dance music will begin, again that of local bands, and issues of theological propriety will be forgotten or at least shelved. Looking back, participants might recall that they had experienced prayer, scripture (projected on the wall) and a sort of communion thingy. Then again, they might not.

This is simply one snapshot from the life of Parallel Universe, a worshipping community in the heart of the city of Auckland. The evening is one of many in which a group of people experiment with the idea of responding to God in a way that gives conscious recognition to their own context and draws on their own cultural resources.

For four years I was part of the planning team for this venture in alternative worship, and they were some of the most wildly exciting years of my life. Now I have changed cities, but have found refuge in a similar experimental community called Soul Outpost. I find it hard to contemplate a life of faith without this invigorating participation in revitalizing worship.

On another memorable evening at Parallel Universe, the theme was 'Enough is Enough'. It was loosely based on Jesus' feeding of the five thousand. The climax of the evening was a small drama, acted out on a raised platform in the centre of the bar tables. Two kiwi blokes, Bill and Jim, were bantering over a barbecue. The Mad Butcher was supposed to turn up with a supply of free sausages, but he hasn't showed. To make matters worse, the truck carrying the beer hit a flyover on the way out. 'Strewth, mate,' says Jim, 'The beer'll be flat!' The situation they face is a crowd of people waiting for sausages and beer, and nothing to give them.

Enter Ben. They quiz him to see if he can help out, but all he has is his lunch, which consists of a meat pie, a can of local beer and a can of cola. He's happy to contribute that if it's any help. They decide they'll just have to make do with what they've got. Jim lifts the pie and can towards heaven and cries out, 'God, me old mate, we'll be snorkelling in the sewage pond if you don't help us out. We ain't got much, but what we've got we give to you.' He breaks the pie in half and opens the two cans, and begins to pass them around. Under each table in the venue, pies and cans have been stashed. Suddenly everyone is eating pies (shared among them) and drinking cans. The atmosphere is amazing.

There was a nice corollary to the event. We had tried to get beer donated from local breweries, but kept being told the amount we wanted was too small. So, eventually, a persistent member of the team hit on the idea of asking for ten dozen and these were given without question. The pies and cola were also donated. At the end of the evening, the planning team was left packing up. There were a whole lot of pies and cans left over. It wasn't until we began dividing them up into cartons for each of us to take home, that we recognized how this paralleled the original event. That set us laughing for a long time.

Contextualization or theatre? Relevance or tackiness? Radical reinterpretation or sacrilege? The line between each of them is thin. The aim of Parallel Universe was clear: we wanted to worship God with our eyes and ears open. Our hope was to be faithful to the Christian tradition in which we stood, while becoming relevant to the culture in which we ourselves participated. Undoubtedly there were failures. At times—the experiment with pies and beer may have been one of them—the desire to connect lured us beyond the limits of decorum. The moments of success, though, were so profoundly liberating, so enormously satisfying and transforming, that all of us have been spoilt for life. We have tasted the possibilities, and this has left us discontent with the religious status quo.

The following reflections are musings arising from the ongoing process of experimentation in worship. They are fragmentary, incomplete and possibly contradictory. A circumnavigation of communion will be the binding thread that holds them together.

WORSHIP AND MISSIOLOGY

The call to form Parallel Universe was informed by a tape passed around interested people by Mark Pierson, an Auckland Baptist minister. It is a recording of a Greenhouse lecture given by Graham Cray on the essential missiological focus of alternative worship. He substantiated this by the notion of crossing cultures; moving from the familiarity of the Church subculture to the new realm of dance culture. Both new worship and Graham himself have moved on significantly since then, but his emphasis on the connection between worship and mission was hugely influential for us at an early stage.

Both our initial conviction and our subsequent discoveries uphold the view that worship is, in and of itself, missiologically significant. There is something in the gathering of the community to make its heartfelt response to God that creates tangible hints of his kingdom. If such occasions are open and accessible to outsiders, they may become points of encounter between those seeking meaning and the living God. A word of qualification is necessary, however. If the events are motivated and planned to be missiological (that is, for others), then they run the risk of not being genuine worship. The focus of worship must never become utilitarian. It is not aimed at, or on behalf of, a 'target group', but must arise from us.

That said, the key to the missiological import of worship is its accessibility. Traditionally, many factors have counted against this—the use of specially designated church buildings, the strong Christian subculture with in-house jargon and the conscious efforts to exclude outsiders in some sections of the Church. The so-called 'fencing of the table' at communion is a particular scandal in this regard, and will merit further comment later. The question, 'Who may participate in worship?' is closely related to the question, 'Who may participate in communion?' For the meantime, it may be worth considering what it is about worship that gives it missionary significance.

In worship, the community is oriented towards God. In this way it invokes, remembers and seeks to participate in the divine presence. The assembled people call from the ambiguity and agony of their daily existence, both summoning and ritually re-presenting the one who has been described as the 'lure of creation'. In some sense, there will be a creative and stylized retelling of the Christian story in the event of worship. There is the hope of connection between the life of God and the life of humanity. Meanings that have been lost sight of might be remembered in this context. The quiet voice of the gospel—so easily drowned out in the cacophony of the demands made of us in our daily lives—may again be heard. Kingdom values, so threatened in the monetarist realm, are once again held up as possibilities for enactment.

If, then, the act of worship is authentic to human experience in its immediate context and if it is accessible to all-comers, whatever their background, then it may become a place of encounter. Whether or not people are transformed, they will at least have found their own reality seen in the context of the claims of God on their lives. In this way, worship is inherently missiological. At worship, humanity most closely approximates its nature and purpose as 'children of the living God'. If there has been a missiological failure of worship in recent times, it is because worship has failed to represent either the welcoming love of God or the peculiar angst of human existence.

A RADICAL APPROACH

TO THE TRADITION

As Maggi Dawn has pointed out, we cannot be faithful to a tradition simply by passing it on from generation to generation. Changing contexts and symbol systems mean that the act of conserving a tradition in its original form may be the best way of guaranteeing its eventual distortion. Maintaining the integrity of a *motif* instead requires that we drive to the heart of it to understand its significance, and then do our best to re-present the same field of reference within our own context. This is a radical approach, in the sense that it is an attempt to reappropriate the roots of a tradition and, in so doing, be faithful to its transmission.

This is what Jesus did so effectively in relation to Jewish scripture, and what led eventually to his crucifixion. His simple statement, 'The sabbath was made for humankind, and not humankind for the sabbath' (Mark 2:27, NRSV), can only be held true on a deep understanding of the intent of covenant and sabbath. Certainly, to orthodox Jewish ears of the time, it sounded blasphemous, and was subversive of the entire religious practice of the day. Time and again, Jesus claimed faithfulness to the law, at the same time as interpreting it so radically that his practice stood out as peculiar and confrontational.

If we are to focus our discussion by reference to communion, then faithfulness to that tradition will require understanding of what it represents in its genesis. As Möltmann has argued, the last supper, which inaugurated the practice of communion, cannot be understood without some reference to the ministry of Jesus that preceded it. The gathering of his disciples around the table in Jerusalem maintained continuity with the table fellowship of Jesus throughout his years of active proclamation. It would be wrong, therefore, to approach the final meal in isolation, and without some appreciation of its broader context. Let us examine one important aspect of that context.

The table at which Jesus often sat was not only a common locus for his teaching, but also in itself a sign of the kingdom he proclaimed. At the table of Jesus, all were welcome and had a place. Against the backdrop of Pharisaic Judaism, this practice was both remarkable and scandalous (Matthew 9:10–13). It transgressed the ritual code of holiness, with its separation of clean and unclean. Sharing food and community with those of dubious character earned for Jesus the reputation of being 'a glutton and a drunkard, a friend of tax collectors and sinners' (Matthew 11:19). Already Jesus' table had become a sign of the coming kingdom, and a symbol of hope and acceptance.

One of the central images of what that kingdom will be like is contained in Jesus' parable in Luke 14:16–21. Here he compares it to a great dinner party, which the invited guests are too busy and preoccupied to attend. The solution? 'Go out at once into the streets and lanes of the town and bring in the poor, the crippled, the blind, and the lame' (v. 21). The table of Jesus is a place of welcome and celebration for outcasts and sinners. It is a foretaste of the messianic feast that presages the kingdom of God. The only thing that will stop someone from belonging there is the self-imposed one of considering themselves too good to mix with such company.

That last meal in the upper room at Passover, even though a ritualized one, recaptures all those other meals. Even the betrayer, Judas, is welcome to participate and dip his hand into the bowl with Jesus. Peter, whom Jesus knows is shortly to deny him, is not excluded from participation either. The same element of anticipating the kingdom of God is present in Jesus' words, 'I will never again drink of this fruit of the vine until that day when I drink it new with you in my Father's kingdom' (Matthew 26:29, NSRV). One central theme, then, of the Lord's supper must be the demonstration of radical inclusion and acceptance that marks the character of the coming kingdom. It is there in the heart of the tradition, and needs to be affirmed in the re-presenting of it.

CREATIVE REINTERPRETATION

In what ways may this tradition be faithfully celebrated in our own context? There are a number of levels at which this might take place. First, and perhaps most minimally, we can adjust our ecclesiastical practice to resonate with the character of Jesus' kingdom. Within a church setting, the Lord's supper or eucharist or mass or communion has become a highly ritualized drama, played out within the confines of the liturgy and worship of the congregation. Though nominally open to the public in general, in effect it is relatively inaccessible. Few outsiders would feel welcome at the stylized table or altar that forms the centrepiece of Christian celebration.

Matters are made much worse by the so-called 'fencing of the table'. Whether this is explicit in the doctrines of certain streams of the Church or implicit in the veiled warnings given in the invitation in others, it represents a scandal and a denial of the Christian tradition. It seems bizarre that a symbol of Jesus' grace and acceptance should have restricted access. Even Paul's warnings to the Corinthians (1 Corinthians 11:27–34), which have provoked a good part of this development, invite participants to self-examination only as a prelude to participation. It is worth remembering too that the problems there arose from a love-feast with ample food and wine for all.

In many ways, our celebration of communion will not be faithful to its origin until our churches become open to outsiders. However, in the meantime it is at least possible to shape and introduce the eucharist in such a way as to recapture the hopeful celebration of acceptance. Some years ago, I produced an introduction to communion for our own congregation that attempted to do something like this called 'Invitation to the Feast':

Come, all you who thirst,
>*all you who hunger for the bread of life,*
>*all you whose souls cry out for healing;*
Come, come to the feast of life.

Come, all you who are weary,
>*all you who are bowed down with worry,*
>*all you who ache with the tiredness of living;*
Come, come to the feast of life.

Come, all you poor,
>*all you who are without food or refuge,*
>*all you who go hungry in a fat land;*
Come, come to the feast of life.

Come, all you who are bitter,
>*all you whose hopes have tarnished into cynicism,*
>*all you who feel betrayed and cannot forgive;*
Come, come to the feast of life.

Come, all you who grieve,
>*all you who suffer loss as a fresh knife wound,*
>*all you who curse the God you love;*
Come, come to the feast of life.

Come, all you who are sinners,
>*all you who have sold the gift that is within you,*
>*all you who toss uneasily in your bed at night;*
Come, come to the feast of life.

Come, all you who are oppressed,
>*all you who have forgotten the meaning of freedom,*
>*all you whose cries cut to the very heart of God;*
Come, come to the feast of life.

Come, all you who are traitors,
>*all you who use your wealth and power to crucify God,*
>*all you who cannot help yourselves;*
Come, come to the feast of life.

Come, all you who are sick,
>*all you whose bodies or minds have failed you,*
>*all you who long above all for healing;*
Come, come to the feast of life.

Come, all you who are lost,
>*all you who search for meaning but cannot find it,*
>*all you who have no place of belonging;*
Come, come to the feast of life.

The table of Jesus is your place of gathering;
>*here you are welcomed, wanted, loved,*
>*here there is a place set for you;*
Come, come to the feast of life.

However, restoring the open character of the Lord's supper is a small adjustment that is probably inadequate to do justice to the radical nature of Jesus' ministry. It would be of greater help to consider a more prosaic interpretation of the open table of

the kingdom. We might usefully reconsider the suggestion from
Jesus mentioned earlier (Luke 14:12–14, NRSV):

> *When you give a luncheon or a dinner, do not invite your friends*
> *or your brothers or your relatives or rich neighbours, in case they*
> *may invite you by return, and you would be repaid. But when you*
> *give a banquet, invite the poor, the crippled, the lame, and the*
> *blind. And you will be blessed, because they cannot repay you, for*
> *you will be repaid at the resurrection of the righteous.*

When I was minister in a small urban church in Auckland, we
organized an annual event that tried to do something like this. It
was called the Formal Dinner and marked one of the highlights
of the church's year. Invitations would be sent out to all the
boarding houses and psychiatric halfway hostels in the district.
It helped that we already had good relationships with the resi-
dents. They were asked to come to a three-course feast, to take
place in the church hall. Weeks of planning went into the event,
at which the members of the congregation were the cooks, waiters and workers. A whole day was often devoted to the decora-
tion of the hall, to turn it into a restaurant that would be in
keeping with whatever the theme happened to be for that year.

The guests would queue up at the door in anticipation. They
would be dressed in whatever finery they could cobble together
for the occasion. The evening would begin with pre-dinner
drinks and nibbles and, before long, the place would be filled
with a cacophony of noise. Eventually our guests would be
seated and waiters in white shirts, waistcoats and bow ties
would commence service. The meal was always as good as we
could make it, with huge helpings and as many seconds as people wanted. Following the meal, there would be dancing, with
a church band providing the music.

It was a time that I always looked forward to. There was
invariably a kind of magic that settled over the hall. Looking
around, there were street people, alcoholics, psychiatric patients

and people on benefit, crowded around tables. Their faces were alight with conversation and the enjoyment of the food. It seemed to me that the colours were brighter, the food more delicious and the air sweeter on such nights. The Spirit of God was conspicuously present, and the kingdom seemed to draw a little closer for the duration of the evening. Nothing Christian was said at a Formal Dinner. No words would have added anything.

A different way of re-presenting communion is to take it outside the walls of a church. On one notable occasion I celebrated the eucharist amid the rubble of a demolished hospital ward. For many years it had been a geriatric ward, but now had been knocked down to make way for a car park. Two members of our congregation—a doctor and a nurse—had worked in the ward. For them, the site held precious memories of people who had struggled and suffered in their battle for health. Many had died in the place, surrounded by the arms and words of their families and friends. The memorial aspect of the communion was deepened by association with these events, symbolically recaptured in the ritual of commemoration.

Exposing the in-house sacrament of eucharist in this way also accentuated its nature as a vehicle of protest against the existing powers. That interpretation was only strengthened by the presence of a couple of security guards, who kept circling the perimeter of the congregation, speaking anxiously into their walkie-talkies. I had written a lament for the event (the ward in question was named Costley Block):

> By the rubble of Costley,
> there we sat down and wept
> when we remembered our heritage.
>
> Brick unloosed from brick,
> and every one a memory
> of loving and healing and dying.

BREAD AND WINE, BEER AND PIES

In this place people fought for life,
confronted death,
were comforted and cared for.

But now health is bought and sold,
and there is no time for holding hands
or hearing stories.

Everything familiar has been struck down,
the wrecking balls have shattered
our memories and our hope.

Not for ourselves only do we mourn,
but for our nation and our people,
our culture and our life.

In Grafton and Golgotha,
the powers that be
are crushing bones and dreams.

God of the cross,
stand once more with your people
against the murderous bureaucrats.

They know not what they do;
forgive them their arrogance,
their razing of the earth in search of progress.

With our brother Jesus,
help us to forgive them
even as they crucify compassion.

But strengthen here your people,
that we may resist the powers of death
until the end of time.

Grant that we may stand
with the broken and dispossessed,
giving voice to their silent rage.

May we face the System and its servers,
announcing its impotence,
naming evil for what it is.

Transform our despair into defiance,
our resignation into resistance,
that we may overcome our fears and live for your kingdom.

Send your Spirit upon us
that we may no longer nod at iniquity,
but in quiet strength oppose it.

Under the shadow of the cross
we pledge ourselves to the vision of Christ,
and to its cost.

From the rubble of reality
we lift our voices in protest and prayer,
calling out for justice and grace.

God of the new, turn our grief to joy
as you strike deep into the heart of history,
bringing life once more from the grave.

In the introduction to the celebration of communion, I deliberately held the cup out and poured some of its contents into the dusty rubble, where it was absorbed as easily as our poor protest. In the larger scale of things our act of resistance made no difference, but in the development of our communal spirituality of defiance it was a powerful moment.

In such instances of reinterpretation, different elements of the tradition are recovered and experienced in ways that break them out of the contempt of familiarity. In so doing, the power that is always inherent in ritual and symbol is brought to bear on issues and experiences thrown up by contemporary existence, rather than simply being domesticated in ecclesiastical incubation. I venture to suggest that much of the scandal that attached to the ministry of Jesus in his day was due to a similar radicalizing of the common tradition that made it accessible and subversive in the context of his culture. From time to time it is useful to remember that the immediate context of the Lord's supper is the impending execution of this man for political reasons.

THE PERILS OF CREATIVITY

Any creative venture is fraught with tension and danger. Things can go wrong, as perhaps the entire saga of creation would have us remember. The sort of creative reinterpretation that underlies the ventures of groups such as Parallel Universe or Soul Outpost constantly runs the risk of descending into the triviality of 'trendy vicar' territory. To do so would be to create the atmosphere of a faintly ludicrous group of Christians desperately trying to match what is happening in the wider society. The penchant of the media for lampooning such ventures provides the basis for dismissing liturgical experimentation as a form of 'trend-chasing' that is unworthy of the historic majesty of the Church.

Certainly the disinterest of people in historic Christianity is not in itself sufficient reason to begin fiddling with its content in an attempt to make it more attractive. That is the liberal approach, so often associated with Friedrich Schleiermacher and his attempt to communicate with 'cultured despisers of religion'.

To be conservative, in the very best sense of the word, is to seek to be faithful in the passing on of what has been inherited. In times when there is a relatively stable culture, this takes no great effort. However, in periods when there is tumultuous cultural upheaval, such as that experienced by Israel in exile, faithfulness to the tradition demands the sort of creative risk demonstrated by Isaiah 40—55. Here we see a reappropriation of the historic legacy that is both consistent with the past yet radically new.

Cultural change raises the searching question of how we can sing the Lord's song in a new land. In such circumstances, the mere repetition of familiar words and practices can lead us to distort that which we are seeking to preserve. Currently, the transition into post-modernity is causing a cultural cyclone in which reiteration borders on blasphemy. Those who debunk the process of reinterpretation because of its risks make the mistake of imagining that there is some alternative. It is too easy an option to become a self-satisfied 'religious despiser of culture'. Certainly, the Christian faith has survived two thousand years and a huge variety of cultural and historic contexts so it is likely to survive this period of history. However, it has survived thus far by virtue of its ability to be flexible, creative and radical in its transmission of the story.

Alternative worship groups such as Parallel Universe and Soul Outpost are fragile attempts to recontextualize the Christian faith within the settings of their participants. One of the discoveries of such communities has been the abiding power and significance of ritual and sacrament. In fact, among the representatives of the emerging culture who tend to frequent these gatherings, there is a great appreciation of that which is dramatized and symbolic, as opposed to the verbal and formulaic. We have discovered a willingness to participate, even at points where comprehension or agreement might be lacking. This means that the eucharist is perhaps more missiologically significant than it has been for some centuries.

In a recent Soul Outpost evening, a labyrinth was set up in a room, complete with many candles, incense and Benedictine chanting. People came from all walks of life: Christians, Buddhists, those with a non-specific interest in spirituality. We provided a guide-sheet to walking the labyrinth that was unashamedly Christian. To one side was a low table set out with candles and the elements of communion, including a loaf of freshly baked bread. Most people took the time afterwards to kneel in that space and eat and drink. There was no leader, no words of explanation, no one even to serve the elements, yet, for many, it was a deeply moving act of encounter between themselves and God. Perhaps the casual inclusion this ceremony offered bordered on the blasphemous. Perhaps the gospel always does. There is no creativity without risk, and no risk without the presence of genuine danger.

RELEVANCE AND IDENTITY

After many years as a Baptist and a clergyman, I have latterly become a Catholic layman. It is a shift, perhaps, from one end of the theological spectrum to the other, and certainly the cause of a great deal of mystification on the part of friends and colleagues. I have not aided them by being relatively inarticulate on my reasons for the transition. It is only with imprecision that I am able to delve into my psyche to report what is happening on that level. I am sure that it was not the theological purity of the Catholic Church that attracted me, opposed as I am to many quite central tenets of Vatican dogma. Equally, I am sure it had something to do with the centrality of the eucharist. After a lifetime of communion being 'tacked on' to worship and, inevitably, over-interpreted in lengthy explanations, I find the pivotal and deeply symbolic nature of the mass a blessed feeding of my soul.

My membership of the Church is of course entirely contra-dictory. Even the eucharist that so profoundly moves me is, theologically, anathema to me because of its exclusiveness. The male priesthood, the hierarchical structure and some of the moral teaching of Catholicism I find repugnant and yet it has become my central point of belonging. Partly, I suspect, because of my enthusiastic involvement with the experimentation ex-pressed through the alternative worship movement, I needed to find 'weight' somewhere in my life as an anchor point. The Catholic Church certainly provides that. When interviewed by a priest as to my reasons for wanting to join the Church, I joked that if I was going to participate in the institutional scandal of the established Church, I might as well come to the mother of them all. It was only half funny.

My own slightly schizophrenic existence between the poles of Catholicism and the alternative worship movement expresses the inherent tension that must exist between identity and rele-vance, and informs any discussion of the relationship of the eucharist to the wider culture. On the one hand, the Christian community needs to know at all times and in all places who it is (and whose it is) and where it has come from. Communion and baptism are surely the central sacraments for affirming our place of belonging and unique identity as the people of Christ. In both, there is a re-narration of the central events of faith, which keeps alive the 'dangerous memory' at the heart of the movement. If we should once lose a clear sense of our own identity, we immediately forfeit any power to proclaim anything to the surrounding culture.

On the other hand, if we isolate the practice of communion from either the broad Christian tradition or the society in which we exist; if we begin to take for granted that our own religious practice is somehow an end in itself, then we lose all connection with the tense and divisive mission of Christ that generated it. To give up on the quest for relevance is as destructive as letting go of the hunger for identity. True Christian existence lies somewhere in the flux generated by these two powerful theological poles. The danger consequent on relevance is that of faithfulness and syncretism; the danger consequent on identity is that of faithlessness and isolation. The cross of Christ reminds us that the struggle to make a way between these forces is not a comfortable one.

I don't for a moment imagine that Parallel Universe or Soul Outpost represents the future of the Church. Neither do I imagine that orthodox Catholicism represents the way ahead. I do believe, however, that unless there is dialogue between the two streams these groups represent, there will be no future for the Christian Church in the West. Christianity is only viable as a *living* tradition.

History teaches us that the very centrality of communion means that it is frequently the subject of heated debate within the Church, and that is not likely to change. The margins and the centre need to be in communication with each other. I suspect the Jerusalem Council reported in Acts 15 provides a model for the way in which reports of experience around the fringes of the movement can influence an understanding of what God is about.

SOME CONCLUDING STORIES

It may be more appropriate to change my mode of discourse to that of narrative now, which is in keeping with new worship ventures. The following stories are offered without explanation, which I am convinced is the proper way for stories to be told. All of them have some bearing on the eucharist.

The first was told by German theologian Helmut Thielicke. As a boy, he liked to venture out on long cycle rides into the countryside. On one occasion, he decided to go on an expedition that would take the whole day. He didn't take any food with him, planning instead to buy something along the way. It was a pleasant day and he enjoyed the ride. Around noon, he arrived in a small village about the same time as hunger pangs set in. In the centre of the town he found a shop with a sign outside. It was a picture of a filled roll. The roll contained lettuce, tomato, gherkin, cheese, salami and pickle. It set his mouth watering. He leaned his bike up against the outside of the shop and went in.

'I'd like one of those rolls that you have pictured outside', he said to the man who came to the counter. The man looked at him, momentarily puzzled.

'Oh, I see,' he said at last. 'I'm sorry—you see, we don't sell food, we just paint signs.'

The second story is one I discovered somewhere and used in *Godzone* (Lion, 1992). There was once a teacher of great faith and insight. Several disciples gathered around him to learn from his wisdom. It so happened that each time the small community met for prayer, the cat would come in and distract them. The teacher ordered that the cat be tied up whenever the community prayed. Eventually, the great one died, but the cat continued to be tied up at worship time. When the cat died, another cat was bought to make sure that the teacher's wishes were still faithfully observed. Centuries passed, and learned treatises were written by scholarly disciples on the liturgical significance of tying up a cat while worship is performed.

Finally, a story from my time as a Baptist minister. It concerns Ian, who could only be described as a rough diamond. He was a straight-talking, hard-drinking man who liked to call a spade a 'bloody shovel'. In mid-life, he came to a point of self-reflection. He had a history of failed relationships and marriages, not unrelated to his affection for drink. Recently he'd got married again, and thoughts about how he might make this union last where others had failed led him to consider the broader question of what life was about. Through a mutual friend, he turned up at Ponsonby Baptist Church on a Sunday morning with his new wife. They sat in the back row beside the door, ready for a quick getaway should anything strange occur.

It happened to be a communion Sunday. Although Ian could not in any sense be considered a churchgoer, he had some residual knowledge of the proprieties surrounding communion. So, when it came to that part of the service, he whispered to Vicky, his wife, that this part was not for them and they'd better leave now. Before they could exit, however, I began the introduction to the eucharist. I made what was my fairly standard invitation, saying that this was the table of Jesus, and that the only qualification for being at it was that you knew yourself to be a sinner. Ian, slightly stunned, turned to Vicky and said, 'That's the first ****ing time I've ever been welcome in a church!' He came and received communion as an act of response to God, and that was his entry into the Christian faith, which he still holds.

5

DOING THE STORY: NARRATIVE, MISSION AND THE EUCHARIST

Sam Richards

MY STORY

William James, renowned physiologist, physician and philosopher all rolled into one, writing at the turn of the century, suggests that 'conversion' falls broadly into two types.[1] Around a third of believers he describes as 'sick-souled': prone to morbidity, to living out a sense of their own wickedness and a divided mind due to unease. For these people, conversion is instant, thereby fitting the teaching of evangelical theology, with a surrender of the old self and rebirth. Up to two-thirds of believers, however, he describes as 'healthy-minded souls', whose religious life stems from their childhood, who are constantly assured of God's love, with no doubts, self-hate or guilt. These people are 'once born', and their conversion is slow and undramatic, a relaxation into truths they have always believed combined with an active search for meaning and purpose.

To illustrate this distinction, I shall tell a little of my own story. My parents had me christened and took me to church as a child—the local parish church. I have a picture from the local paper of the nursery school nativity play in which I was Mary and my best friend was Gabriel. I was also a member of the Brownie pack, which met in the church hall and had church parades. At the age of about seven I joined the choir (a mixture of adults and children) and I remember being paid sixpence for singing at a wedding. When on holiday, we would often go to a service in a cathedral, a marvellous experience of pomp, choral music, hush, candles, grandeur and being on best behaviour.

We moved to a seaside village when I was nine. Here, again, I sang in the choir (this time made up of only children and young people). Although they themselves had been raised going to church, my parents would not have considered themselves 'religious', but, rather, active and faithful members of the local community. They included us children in their community activities—taking us to church was as natural a part of family life as going to the allotment or watching Dad play for a local rugby team. In church they were involved in reading the lessons, acting as sidesmen, founding the women's fellowship, helping with harvest suppers and so on.

By my teens, I was sometimes taking myself to church, for practices or services in which the members of my family were not involved. I was also aware that going to church was not a normal activity for most of my peers. When I was confirmed aged sixteen—a little late by some standards—I remember feeling profoundly disappointed that the bishop needed us to carry a large sign with our names on and that I didn't feel 'different' afterwards—somehow I felt robbed of a sense of 'specialness'. Even so, church continued to be very important to me. After some months of pushing, I was finally allowed to become an acolyte, despite being female (they had run out of boys). By now, I was completely responsible for taking myself to church, for covering my duties on the rota. I was later asked to help put together a couple of 'young people-led services'. I enjoyed thinking through the construction of a service, the first time I had any choice about the hymns sung, prayers said, voices heard.

At the age of eighteen I went off to college. I got involved in the college chapel and an ecumenical group called C20, which gave me my first exposure to both evangelicalism and the idea of mission. It was also my first real experience of a Christian peer group, for my church had no youth group or youth worker and only a couple of teenagers, although some of my friends at school had been members of other churches. I found evangelicals a little full on and at times rather arrogant in their assumption that they were the only *real* Christians or that their way of praying (making it up out loud) was the only real way of communicating with God—particularly when I thought of all the faithful old ladies in church at home! The idea that not everyone had really considered the Christian faith for themselves or experienced God's closeness was something completely new to me—and perhaps set the course for the rest of my life.

Of my faith, I would say I was quite simply a child who had always believed. I went to church, heard the stories and always considered them to be true. I loved singing. I was always a participant in church of the unfolding drama. I loved the words of the liturgy, both Prayer Book and Series Three (without necessarily always understanding them)—it was like poetry to me, solemn and beautiful. I liked the special atmosphere of church, the building, the smell, the fancy dress, the familiar faces. I automatically linked what went on in church with other special moments of intense emotion—like walking the dog at night along the beach, crying after arguing with my family, falling in love. Most of all, I loved communion.

That was why I so wanted to be an acolyte. It meant being in on the action, being at the heart of the mystery. I would process down the aisle, with my candle, following the cross; stand on one side of the Bible with my candle as the gospel was read; kneel before the altar with my candle as the elements were blessed. Best of all, I received communion before the congregation, and could return to sit in my stone recess, my senses full of the scent of incense, taste of wafer and wine, singing of the choir, warmth of the candles, colour of the liturgical season. I was in heaven. I was communing with God. Then the final procession at the end of the service, and being included in the extra liturgy whispered at the back. I always found services without communion a little hollow—they didn't pull me into the mystery. It was as though they had no plot. By contrast, Easter and Christmas were full of story, giving added meaning to communion. Midnight mass thrust Christ's passion into the nativity. Holy Week was a feast of vigil and celebration. Each week we told the story and my faith was nourished.

My story clearly puts me into James' second category. My understanding of my faith has undergone many transformations over the years, but the fact of faith has been practically constant, although not always self-consciously so. My faith has always been framed by the Church and the gospel story, as exemplified by the eucharist. The majority of people today do not have that history of encounter with the Church and the gospel.

At the close of the twentieth century, in the time of so-called 'late modernity' or 'post-modernity', my story is the exception and not the rule. Within the UK, there has been a marked drift from nominal Christianity to 'believing without belonging'[2]— folk or civic religion and agnosticism.

The content of belief, while seen largely as a matter of personal or private choice, is, none the less, shaped as much by the surrounding culture as by the individual believer. The 'drift from the churches'[3] is resulting not just in an increasing number of people with no personal experience of attending church, but as the years pass in a move away from Christian orthodoxy in the beliefs held by most people. Post-Christian 'believing without belonging' loosens the relationship between creed and practice, between an idea of 'truth' and daily life and decisions. The Christian story is allowed as private truth, but not as absolute truth. It becomes just another story, not *the* story. Even if it is believed, it is not expected to have any impact on behaviour or life-choices. There are, after all, many other stories on offer.

The challenge to Christianity, which will only increase in the years to come, is how to tell the gospel story so that it is experienced as truth and not just entertainment, and how to enable hearers of the story to connect it with their lives.

TELLING THE GOSPEL STORY

The gospel is both the story and its telling. Christ's incarnation shows us that the revelatory message and the way it is communicated are a seamless robe. How the story is told has an important impact on the content of the story. Christians must remember that they are guardians and tellers of the story, not the owners of it. The missionary task of the Church is to communicate the story in such a way that the hearers relate to the story, whatever their own cultural background.

Film and TV are, of course, major media for storytelling. Arguably, film is superseding music as a major ingredient in youth culture. Of cinema-goers, seventy per cent are under 25, and that age group accounts for more than half of all video rentals.[4] On TV, soap operas and 'drama documentaries' dramatize 'ordinary life'. News bulletins are written as stories, wildlife documentaries have a narrative imposed on them. Even advertising draws us into plots, sub-plots and characters. So, can film and TV be used to tell the gospel story?

As a child, I remember being transfixed by the film *Jesus of Nazareth* as it was shown over the Easter holidays. I fell in love with the blue-eyed Jesus, and cried my way through six hours of high-class drama. Yet, I was equally transfixed by the *Star Wars* trilogy. Film and TV offer, within themselves, no means for judging between the stories told, other than the manner and skill of the telling:

> It is not so much that... viewers have a short attention span, as critics protest, but rather that they know all the stories already and they are ready to shift their attention to other levels of the film presentation, to glossy colour schemes, rapid-fire editing or dizzying camera movements which challenge their comprehension and intensify their emotional engagement.[5]

This suggests that film or TV as media for telling the gospel story are insufficient, for the audience can all too easily respond to the medium rather than the narrative. In two-thirds of the world, the success of the 'Jesus' film may in part be as much a fascination with the medium as with the message. That it has had more limited success in the Western world tells us more about the sophistication of the audience as moviegoers than it does of their need to respond to the gospel. For, above all, film and TV, with their plethora of storytelling, provide passive entertainment. They engage our senses, our emotions, but, in the end, we know that it is fantasy, that the film-maker has shaped a fantasy world for our entertainment.

Of course, this is not to say that film and TV do not have an impact on the society and individuals that watch them, nor that the Christian community should abandon involvement in the media. Indeed, it is arguably a more influential arena of public life than politics, and one in which Christians should be engaging. There is a deeper limitation to film, however. Implicit in film is an individualist approach to 'meaning-making'. The camera shows us one person's perspective, the director selects

the view for us. By its very nature, it implies a relativism—
someone from another vantage point sees another version of
the story, even a very different story altogether. The medium of
film gives the message that narrative is not ultimate truth, and
that there can be no meta-narrative, no overarching story in
which all else has a place.

What other ways are there of telling the gospel story? Books
are an avenue that the Christian community continues to use,
and use well. Three publications by Christian publishers (*The
Book of God* by Walter Wangerin Jr, Lion, 1998; *The Lion Graphic
Bible* by Jeff Anderson and Mike Maddox, Lion, 1998; and *The
Tabloid Bible* by Nick Page, HarperCollins, 1998) are each excellent retellings of the story. They present the narrative using
forms of storytelling (novel, comic strip and newspaper head-
lines) with which people are more familiar than the traditional
Bible chapter and verse. Hearing it anew in these ways brings
fresh revelation and reinforces faith. The Church needs to keep
re-telling the story for each new generation, to enable them to
make it their story. However, the number of those within
earshot is diminishing. The chances are slim of somebody far
removed from Church contact happening to pick up a Christian book, reading it and believing as a direct result.

An attempt was made in 1993 to reach a much wider audience using the published word. *From Minus to Plus* by German
evangelist Reinhard Bonnke was delivered to every household
in Britain. It was a well-produced booklet, telling the gospel
story and inviting response, yet the audience responded to the
medium and not the message. Posted through the letterbox, it
was received as a piece of junk mail. Indeed, by direct mail
standards, the response was disappointing—perhaps because it
was asking for a type of response beyond the means of the
medium. Junk mail tends to ask us to make a consumer choice,
not a life choice.

EUCHARIST AS STORYTELLING

The Christian community has its own medium—one as old as the story and as new as each retelling: the sacraments. More than any other sacrament, the eucharist tells the gospel story.

It tells how Christ shared his last meal with his disciples before the crucifixion, broke and shared the bread and passed around the poured-out wine, telling them the bread was his body and the wine his blood and asked them to do these same things in memory of him. The eucharist doesn't just proclaim the story, it is a dramatic live re-enactment of the story, using tangible, tactile symbols and inviting the audience to participate actively in the remembering. It does not leave the listeners and hearers as bystanders or voyeurs, but calls them into the story —and therefore makes them potential tellers of it to others. For doing it is inseparable from telling it. Jesus asked the first disciples to 'do this in remembrance of me'—and they in turn retold the story in the enacting, as part of the remembering.

For those first disciples, remembering the stories of God in the living out of faith was a part of their Jewish inheritance. Within Jewish tradition, the verb *zarak*, which means 'to remember', implies recalling the event so that all the power of it is present in the now. In such a way, the Israelites were told to remember the Passover, by participating in it via the telling of it. In the same way, the eucharist is participation in the redemption of the cross.

This pre-literate medium may prove to be the most power-ful available to Christians in an increasingly post-literate age. Now may be the moment for 'new' or traditional non-liturgical churches to consider exploring the place of liturgy and ritual within their worship, so that they are able to offer people ways of participating in the eucharistic story in church. We live in a world that understands spectacle and drama. However, 'If we are asking our contemporary culture to "come and see", we must have something to show them as well as something to say.'[6]

The eucharist provides the Church with both. The informal 'breaking bread' styles of 'new' and house churches may not be enough to enable people to appropriate the meaning of the story. These churches are often excellent in performing the sacrament of baptism in such a way that those present are aware that the experience itself is a landmark in the personal stories of those being baptized, and also an obedient action that joins their stories to that of Jesus. Yet, they are often guilty of sharing bread and wine in a way that assumes everyone knows the story and, therefore, that they are able to access the spiritual resources of the Lord's supper without the act being put into an explicit context of doing and remembering the story.

HEARING THE STORY

It is folly to assume that people know the story. A bright, articulate teenage girl once told me, while comparing jewellery, that her gold cross had a woman on it—mistaking the cloth that tastefully covers Christ's loins for a miniskirt. And a porter at an Oxford college, when asked what time the chapel services were, replied that matins was at nine, and Euro-Christ at eleven. The gospel story is unknown or hidden in technical language. We, as every other generation of the body of Christ, are called to share it, to explain it to those around us.

Story is a carrier of truth, one as old as humanity. When a story of personal experience has been told by someone to a friend, they tell another, who tells another. On the telling to yet another (who has no relationship with the originator), it often becomes a carrier of more than personal truth. Once a story has lived in the telling to this fourth generation, it has moved beyond 'a funny/strange/interesting thing happened to a friend of a friend of mine…'—it has become an 'everyman' story.[7] It is told, and lives on as a story, because, for the teller and hearer, it carries some truth about humanity. Its power no longer depends on personally knowing the person concerned.

The generation growing up within the culture shift we currently know as post-modernity or late-modernity has not really abandoned truth, nor the search for it (unlike some philosophical post-modernists). Rather, the truth for them 'is neither hard-boiled fact nor universal principle; rather, it embraces doubt and ambiguity. To post-modern youth, truth is event—personal, passionate, transcendent. They unapologetically up-end Descartes: "I experience, therefore I know."'[8]

For this new generation—and the new world in which the Church increasingly finds itself—the eucharist offers a story-shaped experience as a carrier of the gospel truth. It may prove to be the most effective arrow in the Church's quiver as it seeks to pierce the hearts of those beyond its reach with the love of the wounded saviour.

Hearing the story also invites us to tell our own story. The telling of personal faith stories, or giving of testimonies, has a place at the heart of the Christian tradition. They are examples for us of how individuals have seen their story within the over-arching gospel story—or meta-narrative. To repeat, this surely is the missionary task—telling the gospel story so that others may seek the purpose of their own stories within it and come to identify the gospel as 'the one short story we feel to be true',[9] telling of life or death, hope or despair, heaven or hell.

Beyond the sharing of 'journey to faith' stories, the Church needs to enable the telling of all people's stories. Contemporary society provides many a therapeutic and pseudo-therapeutic opportunity for telling our stories—from counselling sessions to *Oprah*. For counselling, a person needs to have identified a need for help; for *Oprah*, the person needs to have a story deemed worthy of the TV audience. By contrast, the Church must offer attentive listening to everyone's and anyone's story (not just those seeking aid or fame) as an act of love and service. If faith is seeing our own story within the gospel narrative, committing our story to the one knowable within the old, old story, then the Church has a role to play as both a teller and hearer of stories.

While hearing the stories of others does already have a well-worn place within pastoral ministry, it can appear dislocated from the missionary task. If Jesus is our example, however, the pastoral and the missionary tasks are intimately interwoven. Jesus' healing encounters proclaim the good news that the kingdom of God is at hand. Giving people outside the Church the space to find and tell their stories can be a healing encounter. It can allow long-silenced voices to tell for themselves stories that question and counter those that dominate and oppress them,[10] and, in turn, enable them to discover freedom and wholeness within the stories of faith. For stories are agents of transformation: 'The world changes when we tell different stories about it.'[11] The Christian community, however, must assert that the missionary task is not to make God's story fit with personal stories, but, rather, to discover ourselves narrated into the gospel:

> Narrative theology argues that God's story is logically prior: a consuming text that transforms our misshapen outlook upon reality and enables us to view ourselves and the world from a radically different outlook.[12]

BEING THE STORY

Peter Berger has illuminated the role of 'plausibility structures',[13] those social arrangements that make certain worldviews possible. For instance, a society that denies educational opportunities to its 'underclass' is able to continue in the belief that that race/class/caste/group is obviously less intelligent and therefore best suited to menial tasks, as they are not able to achieve the socially defined level of intelligence—for instance, being able to sign their name or read. The social structures help to create and reinforce the prevailing 'common sense'.

Christianity, as much as any other worldview, needs plausibility structures. Christians need spaces, relationships and experiences that make the gospel a plausible meta-narrative for a life of faith, particularly in the face of a growing 'common sense' or worldview that rules out as impossible exclusive, universal, all-embracing truth.

Bishop Lesslie Newbigin argued that the local congregation should be the 'hermeneutic of the gospel'.[14] Gathered acts of worship, storytelling, liturgy and eucharist, although beautiful, are not enough. Rather, the story has to be lived out by the congregation. They must witness to its nature by their deeds. It is the fruit of the Spirit (Galatians 5:22–23) that demonstrates that the story is being indwelled: 'You will recognize them by their fruit' (Matthew 7:16, REB). Without a worshipping community that gathers around the story, it may not be possible to tell the story to others.

Yet, the tensions here are enormous. The need to sustain the local congregation of believers and the integrity of the gospel in an increasingly hostile context may well drive the Church into myriad well-defended, closed and self-contained worshipping congregations, unable to reach over the walls and moats they have constructed and tell the good news to those outside. Meanwhile, those who are mission-minded become increasingly detached from the Church in their attempts to stay among those who belong to other communities (with alternative plausibility structures and worldviews).

Then these mission-minded believers become unable to sustain the faith from which their missionary impulses sprang because they are denied the support of a worshipping congregation. The challenge faced by the Church is that it is called to do both—to keep the story in faithful remembrance and to share the story in mission. Indeed, the story may hold little truth for a hearer when they see it reflected in the life of a solitary Christian, too easily dismissed as a freak. The hearer needs the context of a plausibility structure, the worshipping community, as much as the teller, in order for the story to make a real impact.

The Church needs to create and support mission communities.[15] In this context, the role of the eucharist may need revision. If the worship is to be incorporated into mission, then it must be open to those as yet outside the community of faith. Indeed, it may seem increasingly foolish to ask people to believe without first having experienced the presence of God in worship, even if God is only experienced as an unknown (Acts 17:23), given that we are in a world where experience counts for more than words. Hence, the experience of sharing in the remembering and telling of the eucharist story needs to be open to those beyond the boundary of the faithful few.

In the New Testament accounts of the last supper, we find Jesus sharing it with the twelve disciples—a chosen few. However, they were chosen by their relationship to Jesus, not for their ability to make sound theological and doctrinal sense of the experience (certainly not at the time it was happening), nor by their faith commitments, for Judas was not excluded from the experience.

In suggesting that the eucharist should be open to those beyond the normal boundaries of committed membership, I am not suggesting a free for all. The story still needs to be told by its guardians, from a position of committed belief, in the act of the eucharist. The story should be shared among those with whom there is a relationship. Indeed, the practice of including young children in the eucharist before they have made a public, personal declaration of faith and Church membership is growing in some quarters[16]—justified in terms of the relationship that exists between those children and the worshipping community.

Likewise, the mission community should be building relationships with those beyond its edges and, on the basis of those relationships (not any prerequisite of faith commitment), extend the invitation to participate in the act that is at the heart of the life of the community—the eucharist. This invitation to an event will find resonances out in today's world. It will also resonate with a traditional invitation within the eucharist for those present who are not full members of a recognized Church to receive a personal blessing (usually involving the laying on of hands) while full members receive the bread and wine. The problem today is that the Church needs to be inviting all people to the eucharistic event in the first place, not just extending to existing spectators an invitation to limited participation within it.

While many Church leaders may find this argument goes too far, I feel strongly that people may need to do the story to hear it—to partake of the bread and the wine. In training settings, role-playing is often used to enable the participants to engage, understand and reconsider their felt responses. Doing something, even if it is only acting or role-playing, changes our understanding of it. Ritual actions are not just carriers of meaning, they also facilitate the personal making of meaning. This invitation to experience the story as an event in the eucharist opens a way for the gospel so that people can respond to it as truth.

CONCLUSION

In just about the only indigenous storytelling culture alive in the UK today—that of the traveller community—relationships are inherent in the communities' storytelling. They say that when you tell a story, the spirit of the person who told it to you stands behind your shoulder. Behind them stands the one who told them the story, and so the line goes back to the originator of the tale. They stand there, poised to poke the teller sharply in the ribs, for two reasons. First, to ensure that the teller does not stray too far from the original story, add too many twists, turns, tangents and personal nuances that it ceases to be the story they were told. Second, to ensure that the teller does not begin to explain or interpret the story, but stays true to the task of telling.[17] The Church would do well to remember this idea for it would remind us that, as we tell the gospel through the eucharist, we stand at the end of a line of tellers that stretches back directly to Christ and the last supper. More importantly, it would remind us that our calling is, first and foremost, to tell the story ourselves.

To tell is to do, to do is to tell. May we live eucharistic lives, sustained by the telling of 'the one short tale we feel to be true'.

6

CHARISMA, FREEDOM AND THE EUCHARIST

Dave Roberts

Members of the charismatic movement—an unruly coalition of disparate theologies united mainly in their belief in the supernatural gifts or 'charisms' of the Holy Spirit for today—are not singing from the same songsheet when it comes to how they observe holy communion (or the Lord's supper or the eucharist or the Lord's table—even the abundance of names for it hints at the problem).

The task of the one who would chronicle the attitudes of charismatic believers to 'holy communion' is a complicated one. Contemporary Church historians have sought to suggest that the nine gifts outlined in 1 Corinthians 12:7–11 have all played a part in Church life through the millennia. Sometimes this may have been in the supernaturalism of the Celtic saints, the ecstatic prophesying of an Anabaptist or a tongues-speaking D.L. Moody, but many would regard charismatic theology as a small tributary in the worldwide Christian stream until the early part of this century. The impact of the worldwide Pentecostal movement that was brought to birth between 1900 and 1908 and is now the largest numerical force in Protestantism is considerable. However, our perception of charismatic attitudes towards the 'Lord's table' will reflect the growth of the 'charismatic movement' from the late 1960s until the present day.

This movement impacted the mainline denominations throughout the Western world, and was pioneered in the UK by Michael Harper, Tom Smail, David Watson, Colin Urquhart, Jim Graham (Baptist) and Rob Frost (Methodist). Also identified with the 'charismatic movement' were the so-called 'house churches'. Key figures in their foundation had their roots in the Christian Brethren (Arthur Wallis, Denis Clark), but many others arrived from the Salvation Army (worship leader Dave Fellingham, music producer Les Moir) and other Pentecostal or Wesleyan groups.

Standing back to evaluate charismatic attitudes to communion, freedom and charismatic gifts, they fall into three distinct groups.

Renewed liturgical traditions: The numerically large Anglican grouping that often forms up to thirty to forty per cent of any cross-denominational charismatic gathering, such as Spring Harvest.

Strong Lord's supper tradition: Those whose beginnings were in the Christian Brethren tradition. Figures with roots in this movement are often in leadership roles. The Christian Brethren practice of celebrating the 'Lord's supper' every week has shaped their thinking.

Little or no communion tradition: Those in this group have not denigrated the communion service as much as they have simply neglected it or else not invested much time, thought or energy into it.

While attitudes towards communion or the eucharist may be influenced by attitudes towards set liturgical formulae, they are also significantly shaped by stances on the Bible—is it a rule book or a guide book?—and the role of the symbolic, where traditional free church thought has been coloured by a deep suspicion of the earthly and the visual.

With this in mind, it's also worth noting that charismatics are often used to defying convention for their beliefs. While their name is derived from their desire to be used by the Holy Spirit as bringers of God's gifts or charisms, their attitude towards communion is not shaped by their theology of the Holy Spirit's gifts, as much as it is founded on being willing to question tradition and innovate.

To best understand how different wings of the movement approach and understand communion, we should seek to understand the forces that have shaped each group, in both the distant and recent past of Church history. It will also become clear that a major realignment is taking place as articulate voices call the liturgists to carefully integrate freedom into their structured services, even while bored and listless charismatics stumble towards liturgical structure as an antidote to a meandering approach to worship, which breeds faddism or a simple pursuit of excitement.

LITURGICAL CHARISMATICS

The parish vicar faces many dilemmas. How can he facilitate the 1662 traditionalist, the evangelical traditionalist enamoured by the sturdy poetry of Michael Baughen or Timothy Dudley-Smith and the Holy Spirit-hungry innovators?

Alongside all the other factions shaping the Anglican mind are the influences of class and culture. Has Graham Kendrick been acceptable in this context because of the hymnic structure of his songs? Were John Wimber and the Vineyard worship acceptable to many because, like the Fisherfolk's unadorned folk music, they offered many gentle songs that touched cultural nerves conditioned by plainsong and contemplative reflection? While the pragmatists may have been urging a speedy embracing of the new up-tempo pop worship, for some Anglican charismatics it all felt like that distinctly non-middle-class enthusiasm characteristic of Pentecostalism.

In the midst of all this, the vicar must consider how the congregation will remember together the death of Jesus in the meal that he commanded we repeat in remembrance of him. Ten or twenty years ago, the vicar may have thought of himself as a charismatic Anglican, a minority in a cosmopolitan denomination. Because the evangelicals, of whom the charismatics are a subgroup, have come to be the main providers of ministry candidates and found a new confidence, this same vicar may now be thinking of himself as an Anglican charismatic, no longer seeking to observe the letter of liturgical law. He may be sneaking in times of worship or opportunities to exercise spiritual gifts, but now want to give equal weight to both form and freedom.

John Leach, Director of Anglican Renewal Ministries, is an articulate exponent of this tradition. His own gentle revolt against the idea that only the spontaneous will do is captured in his reflection on Psalm 103. He was reminded afresh one day how he was part of a historical continuum:

> I could picture myself joining with the Israelite community in the Temple in Jerusalem, being there as a young boy called Jesus learned the words with his father Joseph, attending a Mass celebrated by Thomas Becket (my favourite historical character) in Canterbury Cathedral, and so on down the ages until I arrived in an urban parish in the Midlands at the end of the twentieth century, still using the same words. Our worship can be greatly enriched if we get in touch with other worshippers, both worldwide and down the ages, by sharing with them in the liturgy.[1]

Leach expresses a strong desire for order and purpose and uses the communion service as an example, reflecting that the purposeful nature of it may act more powerfully in allowing the Spirit to speak:

*In the Communion Service we come into God's presence, acknowl-
edging the help we need even to do that, we get right with him
after all the wrong things which have been a part of our lives over
the past week, we listen to his word read and explained, we bring
to him our needs in intercession, and we approach his table to
receive the bread and wine which will strengthen us to go out and
live for him during the coming week. There is a sense of logical flow
which, when removed, can make services which are supposedly
'open to the Spirit' seem just a bit arbitrary in the way they happen. To put our worship in this kind of framework so that we journey through it, and so that past, present and future are integrated
in a logical way, can be very helpful.*[2]

He offers an example of liturgy and liberty involving the proper
preface that forms part of the eucharistic prayer. He notes that
encouraging the use of familiar phrases such as 'And now we
give you thanks during a time of open prayer' enabled him to
involve many of the congregation in spontaneous prayer while
retaining a liturgical and purposeful feel. John is realistic but
hopeful about charismata and freedom and offers the helpful
insight that liturgy can either be like a cage or a scaffold, a
prison or a climbing frame.

While John may be considered by some to be the voice of
thoughtful Low Church evangelicalism, there have been some
important explorations of liturgical structures by the growing
'alternative worship' movement. While some will view these
through the lens of the sadly misguided activities of the
Sheffield-based Nine O'Clock Service (NOS), the moral failure
of Chris Brain should not obscure the liturgical realities at
work. When asked if NOS was not simply 'Taizé with a drum
machine', Brain acknowledged a debt to, and exploration of,
High Church and Anglo-Catholic liturgy.

Those involved in the NOS were not the only people to
explore this terrain. Youth for Christ worker and Anglican

Jonny Baker led communion at Worship Together '97. Delegate feedback on the Grace service, with its swirling rhythms and five-senses exploration of faith, ranged from the mildly shocked to the 'restored my understanding of liturgy and holy communion'. Other musicians, including Anglican ordinand Maggi Dawn and the Glasgow-based Late, Late Service, have also sought to explore liturgical forms via the eucharist.

When we examine the response of non-liturgical traditions to communion and charisma, we will reflect on the memorialism that has its roots in the teaching of Huldrych Zwingli. Contemporary liturgical tradition seeks to address this rather limiting view of communion as they seek to explore the idea that the whole service declares the word of God.

Robert Webber, perhaps one of the most thoughtful writers on worship we have, writes of a liturgical and symbolic drama. Seizing the opportunity presented by a worship conference attended by a diverse group, he had the vigorous charismatics lead worship for the 'entrance'. The second movement was the 'Service of the Word', which involved scripture readings, storytelling and exposition.

The next step was to respond with thanksgiving. Webber gives the example of a Presbyterian church that understood the 'Lord's table' to be a response and celebration of the word—not a funeral dirge:

> The ancient motif of celebrating the Resurrection has been restored through hymns and choruses. Singing together is a mysterious form of communication that helps us to truly experience the presence of God and his transforming power that means healing and restoration through Christ. [3]

Webber also notes the healing prayer practice of some liturgical churches as a part of the communion service and offers the reflection of one Presbyterian minister:

> 'It is one of the single most important aspects of the ministry here.

*A lot of broken lives are touched. People look forward to that spe-
cial opportunity for prayer, and God is healing the lives of many
through that sacred action.' When we come to God in a state of
vulnerable openness, God breaks through and touches our lives.
This happens especially at the Table of the Lord.*[4]

Youth worship specialist Patrick Angier identifies the human
needs and yearnings that are provoking a renaissance in worship, which is often founded on renewing the liturgy of the
communion meal. He describes a series of searchings:

*The search for community: where we can share and care for one
another even when that means pain and sacrifice.*

*The search for acceptance: where I can be me and still be welcomed
and included.*

*The search for authenticity: where no one has to or is pretending,
where there is a realness to the spiritual that is more than skin deep.*

*The search for sacred space: a place that is holy, where the reality
of God can be experienced, through the senses and with the silence.*

*The search for spiritual growth: where the growth within me is part
of a deepening relationship with God.*[5]

Angier describes how the thanksgiving motif and the search for
a sacred space finds expression at the Awesome service. The
service attracts over eight hundred people and happens on mul-
tiple stages with video screens and lighting transforming the
building. The evening opens with a time of confession and
includes symbolic candles of forgiveness and inclusive up-
tempo worship. You can bounce on a bouncy castle, tie a prayer
knot, relax with boot painting and friendship bracelets in the
hippy house or listen to the band's opening set before getting
back to the worship area to hear the Archbishop being interviewed. Angier comments:

*As the evening reaches the consecration and distribution, the focus
becomes obvious: light and sound draw people to the act of*

communion itself, before an explosion of praise and celebration
sends them out to live and work to God's praise and glory.[6]

What, then, can we conclude about the liturgy and liberty
movement? Webber, Leach and the alternative worship pio-
neers exemplify a new deliberateness. They flow against the tide
of contemporary worship practice by considering themselves to
be worship leaders rather than musicians. The Worship
Together '99 conference saw Leach and liturgist Mark Earey
combine with worship leader Matt Redman to stunning effect,
with the spoken liturgy sparking unplanned and unsolicited
cheering from the congregation.

However, they are not content to simply use contemporary
musical idioms or clumsily insert times for charismatic 'freedom'. Instead, they are affirming the overall structure of the
liturgy, its symbolic power and its sense of order and continuity. They avoid the legalism that says not one jot or tittle can be
moved or changed, and introduce new musical forms and
opportunities for spontaneous contribution. *Patterns for Worship*[7]
is a case in point, suggesting that various service elements
should always be present, but allowing great flexibility regard-
ing which specific items are appropriate at any given time.

Being articulate about why change is being introduced, and
sensitive to the strengths of the past, is more likely to win over
a waverer than a simple appeal to a need for modern methods
or freedom for the Spirit to flow. This is the hallmark of this
new breed of charismatic liturgist.

THE ANTI-LITURGISTS

While the non-conformist, non-liturgical charismatics may
be classified as those *with* a strong communion tradition (ex-
Brethren) and those without (most others), they will have often

drunk from the same philosophical wells. Before exploring the new directions they are taking, it's perhaps instructive to look at what has shaped their antipathy to liturgy and symbol.

For some it is merely one worship ordinance among many. Eleanor Kreider, reflecting on Pentecostalism, reminds us that, for many, it is but one of the situations in which the Spirit might be made manifest: 'Foot washing, healing, and baptism stand together with the Lord's Supper as scriptural ordinances which edify the community.'[8]

Robert Webber expresses the restraint that many feel simply because their tradition has not allowed anything but the most elemental symbols to be part of their worship experience:

'The plainer, the better' attitude determined my view of various symbols in worship. At that time I did not understand that these symbols could be understood as pointing to sacred actions through which an encounter with Christ occurred. I had been taught not to trust Christian symbols. I saw them as symbols of my action, not Christ's action. I came to the waters of baptism to make a public commitment of my faith. I came to the bread and wine to recall Christ in my mind.[9]

In his mind they became little more than memory aids. The reduction of the communion to a simple memory jogger and the fear of liturgical drama are rooted in two key non-conformist beliefs.

One is the purist belief that worship should proceed only from the heart. Repetition or read prayers smacks of a lack of passion. Lurking in the background is a fear that the set forms of liturgy will become idolatrous and equated in people's minds with the Bible.

Allied to this approach is a dualistic view of spirituality. This elevates the mind (evangelicals) or the spirit (many others) as the conduit through which God works to the complete detriment of most of the five senses. The Hebrew mindset would suggest that we can comprehend and understand God and his works via sight, smell, hearing and teaching. (A short walk through the book of Psalms will illustrate this.) The Greek, platonic mindset values the mind and the mystical to the detriment of the earthly and things of the flesh, which have been corrupted and are impure. Those raised in this tradition may well be wary of the imagination, fearful that symbols will become icons and then idols.

Caught in the undertow of this is the guilt by association that links the liturgists with those who hold to doctrines of the 'real presence' of Jesus in the elements. New Church leader Derek Brown makes his case against 'real presence' theology, suggesting that it leads directly to a worship of the elements 'as if they were Christ Himself'. He also says that it leads to a communion-centred salvation, rather than a cross-centred one. He goes on to quote J.C. Ryle and Thomas Cranmer as opponents of the doctrine.[10]

Brown's recognition that not all in the liturgical tradition embrace transubstantiation is helpful, but for many these views and the liturgical drama of High Church mass are so interwoven that anything out of the ordinary gets brushed aside as being the short end of the 'real presence' wedge.

Many are still wedded to the Zwinglian notion of memorialism, which is ably described in the Brethren worship symposium *Declare His Glory*:

> For Zwingli, the purpose of the Lord's Supper was to stir up our memory of Christ so that we might feed on him spiritually through faith according to the teaching of Christ recorded in John 6. Through this feeding on him, we will also be united to one another as Paul teaches in 1 Corinthians 10:17.[11]

We may *remember* Christ, but can we fail to *encounter* him? Are we in danger of being left with what contemporary theologian Wayne Grudem calls 'a doctrine of the real absence'?

In the light of this possibility, many charismatics are running a slide rule over their worship practices once again, defending the possibility of spontaneous contribution, but seeking a new place for liturgical formula and symbolic communication. At the core of this, for many, is a fresh examination of the communion service.

New Church leaders Chris Seaton and Roger Ellis are seeking a 'balanced concern for scholarship, the Bible and spirituality'. This has led them to explore symbolism and liturgy. They call for new liturgies that will engage dynamically with contemporary culture:

> We are whole human beings, so in order to perceive God fully it is not a case of us encountering him only with our minds or even just with minds and emotions. There are other senses like smell and taste which can further adorn the body of God's truth. If this were not so, the 'breaking of bread' would not need to be participated in, merely talked about! We believe that in this generation and culture, many churches will have to reassess their attitude towards liturgy and symbolism. [12]

Webber meets many others on a similar pilgrimage. Why were so many dismissing rich traditions of worship? Why was there a relentless pressure to constantly innovate? One pastor, Doug Mills, concluded that some of the traditions must have been inspired by the Spirit and began to make changes. He scheduled the Lord's supper on a regular basis, included a psalm and more scripture readings and began to follow the Christian calendar:

> Our worship has become fuller and deeper... We are realizing the significance of being a part of God's universal church... We are becoming a less selfish people... Our people are characterized by a healthy 'fear of the Lord' [and] we have been able to continue to learn and develop in the area of worship without losing the life and vitality of the Holy Spirit. [13]

What can we conclude about the attitude of the traditionally anti-liturgical elements in Church life? While some remain locked into fairly meaningless 'remember and repent' services, some are making a theological shift that involves them in a greater appreciation of symbolism, spiritual encounter and the role of all our senses in worship.

In the light of this, it is instructive to look at other trends that are influencing charismatic thought and, in turn, will influence perceptions of liturgy, freedom and the breaking of bread.

CELL CHURCH AND COMMUNITY

The charismatic tune currently being whistled everywhere concerns the idea that there should be an active 'church' for every 1000 people in the nation. Closely allied to this is a growing belief that discipleship requires the close friendships of two or three others, the companionship and debate of a group of nine to twelve, the community of 70 to 100 and the resources and inspiration of a larger group at special times. There is a special focus at present on the role of the small group as the day-to-day expression of the Church.

This provokes a serious examination of everyday spirituality, influenced in various ways by Messianic Jews, the Celtic tradition and the 'Earth is the Lord's and everything in it' approach popularized by the late Francis Schaeffer. It's not too long before this line of logic causes you to examine the role of meals in the Gospel narratives. They occur at many key moments, including the first miracle (the water into wine at the wedding), eating with Zacchaeus (rejecting sectarianism), eating with publicans (rejecting separatism), the Passover meal, a meal of fish prepared by the risen Lord for the disciples and a meal with the two disciples in Emmaus, among others.

The liturgist and the charismatic discover a rich vein once

they begin digging for the gold in this scriptural mine. Part of this comes from exploring the roots of the Lord's supper in the Passover meal. The Passover meal, a symbolic remembrance of deliverance from Egypt, foreshadowed our deliverance from the bondage of sin by Jesus.

Derek Brown explores this in *Bread and Wine*, quoting author Giovanni Papini as he describes the banquet that symbolizes the hasty repast of the Israelite fugitive:

A lamb or kid was cooked in the quickest way, which was roasted before the fire. Bread was baked without yeast, for there was no time to wait for the dough to rise. They must eat in haste, staff in hand, with their loins already girded and shoes upon their feet, as if they were to set forth on a journey. The bitter herbs represent the coarse, wild vegetables the fugitives snatched by the way to still the pangs of hunger on that pilgrimage. The reddish sauce wherein they dip their bread is to remind them of the bricks the Jewish slaves had been forced to make for Pharaoh. The wine is an addition; it represents the joy of escape, the promise of the longed-for vine, the intoxication of gratitude to the Almighty. [14]

These words help us to understand the element of celebration, the freedom, the gratitude that was part of the Passover meal and which we are to enjoy in the Lord's supper.

Brown further explains the liturgical sequence involved in the meal, reminding us of the four cups of wine that were to be drunk during the meal: the cup of sanctification, the cup of celebration of the lamb, the cup of thanksgiving and the cup with closing prayers. After the meal, Jesus and the disciples sang a hymn. This hymn, part of the Passover meal, was the great 'Hallel', based on Psalms 114—118, and was to be sung to a 'rollicking melody'.

Eating together is key in establishing, maintaining and transforming relationships such as those that are at the root of the cell church concept. The Jewish tradition invests the whole of life with the possibility of thanksgiving, but also affirms rituals and liturgies that aid that process. Webber says of one such meal:

> *What we were involved in was more than a meal, it was a ritual— a religious ritual—that had power to unite a family, recall history, create reverential awe, shape values, and provide a focal point to which memory for both parents and children will return again and again.* [15]

As these ideas are explored and Christians become involved in their communities and with their non-believing neighbours, issues of justice inevitably arise. Social compassion has been a hallmark of revival movements. Just as Paul warned the Corinthians about the abuse of social privilege at the communion meal, it may also be wise to remind the socially minded charismatic of the unity and breaking down of barriers that happen as people eat together.

EVANGELICALS AND THE ARTS

Anglicanism, with its consensual approach and porous boundaries between differing theological camps within its ranks, was always a safer haven for the Christian artist than nonconformism. The Church was the seedbed for much classical music and encouraged the visual arts via Church architecture and religious art.

Much of the impetus for the contemporary worship and Christian music genres came from within the ranks of nonconformism, however, and was often driven by a pragmatic desire to 'reach the lost' or 'keep the kids'.

As the movement matured during the 1970s and 1980s, there was a growing desire for a mature biblical approach. For some, this led them away from an Augustinian 'is it described in clear detail?' blueprint approach to scripture and towards a more Lutheran 'does it contradict key biblical ethical wisdom?' questioning. It became clear that the Bible often advocated symbolism (Agabus binding the apostle) or commanded dance (Psalms 149—150), and that a thoroughgoing examination of scriptural metaphor, image, poetry and symbols would lead gently away from the sterile plainness of much non-conformist, cerebral-orientated worship.

The fruit is a generation growing up in the Church with a richness of colour, variety of sounds and open to movement, dance and visual symbolism. While this has no direct bearing on liturgy or the Lord's table, it does provide a climate in which systemization of these symbols into liturgical forms will provoke little resistance as long as freedom for personal expression remains. If liturgy is thought of as helpful structures, rather than a rigid, centrally imposed ritual, then there is an even greater openness.

Perhaps one of the most significant champions of this has been Graham Kendrick, who has produced liturgical-style praise march structures that retain the possibility of personal prayer and proclamation by the participating individuals.

SYMBOLISM AND THE
WORD OF GOD

The process discussed above is aided by a growing body of writing about the role of the symbolic. Webber writes of his visit to a church where the eye-gate was appreciated:

On the left side of the table, perched against an earth-toned water pot from the first century, was a striking crown of thorns with its ugly and cruel thorns quite visible. In front of the crown of thorns were several large, cruel-looking spikes and, to the

*right, a money bag for the thirty pieces of silver. To the right of
these symbols of the Passion stood a striking bowl of fresh green
and red grapes. Slightly to the right but a little behind them was
a chalice and, in front of that, a freshly baked loaf of bread on a
paten. A small pitcher for the wine stood nearby. To the far right
was a basin for washing feet. Behind the basin was a large
earthen pitcher with a towel draped over the handle. To the left
of the water vessel, behind all the other objects were stalks of
wheat, palm branches, and a long stick with hyssop on the end.
Before my eyes, the entire Passion was brought to me, and I
encountered Jesus.* [16]

Webber integrates his own response to those symbols with an
expectation that he will be renewed afresh by the Holy Spirit
whenever he comes to the table. He reflects that he has sought
confirmation of the Christian faith in knowledge (evidence that
demands a verdict) and experience ('I know he lives because he
lives in my heart'), but concludes that nothing has had such a
profound impact as the work of the Holy Spirit, who confirms
the truth of Christ for him at the table of the Lord.

Webber, like others, is integrating personal prayer for healing
into the liturgical process of holy communion, inviting people
to receive prayer after they have partaken of the bread and
wine.

Brethren writer Alan Palmer, commenting on the possibility
of an encounter with God in the communion meal, calls for a
'receptionism'. He reminds us that the Anglican scholar Roger
Beckwith has defined this as the belief that 'Christ is truly
received, though without any change (except in use) in the elements'. [17]

We are seeing the birth of a movement. It is by no means a
mass movement, but it may yet come to have huge sway in the
worldwide Church. Robert Webber is the scribe of this movement and sets out its creed as follows. The manifesto below

reflects his thought, if not his exact words, as he calls for the integration of charisma, freedom and the eucharist.[18]

A restored commitment to the sacraments, especially the Lord's table. Webber calls us away from mere dispassionate 'obedience' and towards a recognition that symbols can be used as a point of contact between people and God. The Lord's presence and power are released in these acts as the worshipper encounters God in water, bread and wine.

An increased motivation to know more about the early Church. What New Testament principles were applied by those who were discipled by the twelve, and by those who followed them?

A love for the whole Church and a desire to see the Church as one. Webber eloquently promotes unity amidst diversity:

> Convergence churches appreciate the gifts that each stream of the Church provides to the whole. Each church approaches convergence from a unique point of view. A church does not necessarily have to change its identity when it becomes a part of a convergence movement.

An interest in integrating structure with spontaneity in worship. Liturgies are being reintroduced into the Church to bring a balance in worship among all the elements that scripture has revealed as necessary for worshipping God in spirit and in truth. Webber reminds us that in using liturgical elements, worship becomes the work of 'the body in praise, repentance, the hearing of the word, and the celebration of Christ's death and resurrection' and that this does not preclude the spontaneous moving of the Spirit.

He goes on to note the increased use of the Apostle's Creed

and the Nicene Creed, and their role in affirming the foundational roots of orthodoxy. What particularly strikes him however is that:

The Lord's Supper is being celebrated with a greater understanding of the sacredness of the event, and churches are following the Christian year and liturgical calendar more consistently as a means of taking congregations on an annual journey of faith.

A greater involvement of sign and symbol in worship. We are reclaiming the arts for Christ, using signs and symbols that point beyond themselves to a greater truth. These symbols serve as contact points for apprehending inward spiritual reality.

A continuing commitment to a personal salvation, biblical teaching, and the work and ministry of the Holy Spirit. Innovation and rediscovery do not mean the abandonment of a stream but a convergence of streams.

This convergence may yet prove to be the prophetic act by the Church in the new millennium that will end some of the either/or sectarianism that has so hampered Church growth.

REFERENCES

INTRODUCTION

1. Roger Palms, *The Jesus Kids* (SCM Press, 1971), p. 7.

2. Billy Graham, *The Jesus Generation* (Hodder & Stoughton, 1971), p. 11.

RHYTHM OF THE MASSES

1. 'Dancing to a new expression' from the album *Grace*, Proost, 1997.

2. On 'filling up an empty ritual', see Eleanor Kreider, *Communion Shapes Character*, Herald Press, 1997, pp. 159–62).

3. Kreider (op. cit.) traces the development of the eucharist.

4. See R.C.D. Jasper and G.J. Cuming, *Prayers of the Eucharist*, 3rd edition (Pueblo, 1987) for a good range of early eucharistic prayers.

5. Jasper and Cuming, op. cit., pp. 82–87.

6. Pete Ward, *Worship and Youth Culture* (Marshall Pickering, 1993), p. 88.

7. Maggi Dawn in Graham Cray et al., *The Post-Evangelical Debate* (Triangle, 1997), p. 39.

8. Stanley Hauerwas, 'The Gesture of a Truthful Story' in

Jeff Astley, Leslie J. Francis and Colin Crowder, eds, *Theological Perspectives on Christian Formation* (Eerdmans, 1996), p. 102.

9. Maggi Dawn, in Cray et al., op. cit., pp. 53, 41.

10. Karl Rahner, *Theological Investigations*, vol. I, trs. C. Ernst, 1961, 1965, p. 153.

11. Helmut Thieliche quoted by Graham Cray in a lecture on 'Youth congregations', Youth for Christ staff conference, 1997.

12. Andrew Walker, *Telling the Story* (SPCK, 1996).

13. See, for example, Walker, op cit., pp. 13–14; N.T. Wright, *The New Testament and the People of God* (SPCK, 1992), pp. 97–98, 132; Tom Sine, *Live It Up* (Herald Press, 1993), pp. 72–89; Richard Middleton and Brian Walsh, *Truth Is Stranger Than It Used To Be* (SPCK, 1995), p. 182; Walter Brueggemann, *The Bible Makes Sense* (revised edition) (Saint Mary's Press, Christian Brothers Publications, 1997), pp. 39–43.

14. Mike Yaconelli in a lecture entitled 'Theology of youthwork', Brainstormers training conference, November 1998.

15. Wright, op. cit., p. 90.

16. Wright, op. cit., pp. 140–143.

17. Middleton and Walsh, op. cit., p. 183.

18. Anglican report, *Youth a Part* (National Society/Church House Publishing, 1996), p. 25.

19. *Youth a Part*, p. 34.

20. Lyotard in *The Post-Modern Condition*, University of Min-

nesota Press, 1984) makes the case that no 'grand story' can claim assent.

21. Mike Riddell, *Threshold of the Future* (SPCK, 1997), p. 106.

22. Walker, op. cit., p. 197.

23. Tom Beaudoin, *Virtual Faith* (Jossey-Bass, 1998).

24. Thanks to Andy Harrington for this expression.

25. The image and story were printed in *The Guardian* in October 1998.

26. John Tinsley, in Astley *et al.*, op. cit., p. 92.

27. In Astley et al., op. cit, quoting Maurice Wiggins, *The Sunday Times*, 10 January 1971.

28. Walter Brueggemann, *Finally Comes the Poet* (Fortress Press, 1989), p. 6.

29 Kreider, op. cit., p. 37.

30. G. Wainwright, *Doxology* (Epworth Press, 1980), p. 26. Quoted by Jeff Astley in Astley et al., p. 245.

31. Pete Ward, *Youthwork and the Mission of God* (SPCK, 1997), p. 134.

32. Beaudoin, op. cit., p. 149.

33. Vincent Donavon, *Christianity Rediscovered* (SCM Press, 1978, 1982), pp. 119–128.

34. Dawn in Cray *et al.*, op. cit., p. 48.

35. The St Hilda Community, *The New Women Included* (SPCK, 1991, 1996).

36. N.T. Wright, *New Tasks for a Renewed Church* (Hodder &

Stoughton, 1992), p. 106; Walker, op. cit., pp. 197–198.

37. Walter Brueggemann, *The Bible and Post-modern Imagination* (SCM Press, 1993), p. 25.

38. Tissa Balasuriya, *The Eucharist and Human Liberation* (SCM Press, 1977), p. 2.

39. Sine, op. cit., p. 67.

PARABLE AND ENCOUNTER

1. Anglican–Roman Catholic International Commission, *The Final Report* (CTS/SPCK, 1982), p. 21.

THE EUCHARIST AND THE

POST-MODERN WORLD

1. Michael Vasey in *The Renewal of Common Prayer*, Liturgical Commission, Michael Perham, ed. (SPCK, 1993), p. 90.

2. Jacques Derrida, *On Grammatology* (Johns Hopkins, 1976), p. 158.

3. Jacques Derrida, 'Living On'/'Border Lines', in *Deconstruction and Criticism* (Routledge and Kegan Paul, 1979), p. 84.

4. David Lyon, 'Memory and the Millennium' in *Grace and Truth in the Secular Age*, Timothy Bradshaw, ed. (Eerdmans, 1998), p. 285.

5. Jean François Lyotard, *The Postmodern Condition* (Manchester University Press, 1984), p. 76.

REFERENCES

6. Douglas Coupland, *Generation X* (Abacus, 1992), p. 126.

7. Jean-Pierre de Caussade, *Sacrament of the Present Moment* (Harper & Row, 1982).

8. Mike Featherstone, *Postmodernism and Consumer Culture* (Sage, 1991), p. 126.

9. David Harvey, *The Condition of Postmodernity* (Blackwell, 1990), p. 286.

10. Harvey, op. cit.

11. Zygmunt Bauman, *Intimations of Postmodernity* (Routledge, 1989), p. 225.

12. Krishan Kumar, *From Post-industrial to Postmodern Society* (Blackwell, 1995), p. 81.

13. See Guy Debord, *Comments on the Society of the Spectacle* (Blackwell Verso, 1997); John Urry, *The Tourist Gaze* (Sage, 1990); Norman Denzin, *The Cinematic Society: The Voyeur's Gaze* (Sage, 1995).

14. Anthony Giddens, *The Consequences of Modernity* (Polity, 1990), p. 53.

15. Jean Baudrillard, *The Transparency of Evil* (Verso, 1993), p. 145.

16. Walter Brueggemann, *Israel's Praise* (Augsburg Fortress, 1988), p. 1.

17. Christopher Cocksworth, *Evangelical Eucharistic Thought in the Church of England* (Cambridge University Press, 1993), p. 190.

18. Charles Taylor, *Sources of the Self* (Cambridge University Press, 1989).

19. Kenneth Stevenson, *Handing On* (Darton, Longman & Todd, 1996), p. 128.

20. Petta Sulkennen, *Constructing the New Consumer Society* (Macmillan, 1997), p. 6.

21. *The Face* Magazine.

22. Bauman, op. cit., pp. xxii–xxiii.

23. Grace Davie, *Religion in Britain Since 1945* (Blackwell, 1994), p. 3.

24. Taylor, op. cit., p. 521.

25. David Stancliffe, 'Evangelism and Worship' in *Living Evangelism*, Jeffrey John, ed. (Darton, Longman & Todd, 1996), p. 26.

26. Alan Torrance, *Persons in Communion* (T.&T. Clark, 1996), p. 312.

27. Iain Banks, *A Song of Stone* (Abacus, 1997), p. 275.

28. Torrance, op. cit., pp. 314, 413–414.

29. Christopher Cocksworth, unpublished paper.

30. B.A. Gerrish, *Grace and Gratitude* (T.&T. Clark, 1993), p. 138.

31. Cocksworth, *Evangelical Eucharistic Thought in the Church of England*, p. 207.

32. Gerrish, op. cit., p. 139.

33. Cocksworth, *Evangelical Eucharistic Thought in the Church of England*, p. 201.

34. David Ford, *Self and Salvation* (Cambridge University Press, 1999), p. 154.

35. Cocksworth, *Evangelical Eucharistic Thought in the Church of England*, p. 209.

36. Cocksworth, *Evangelical Eucharistic Thought in the Church of England*, p. 221.

37. Alan Kreider, *Worship and Evangelism in Pre-Christendom* (Grove, 1995), p. 8.

38. Bryan Spinks, 'Liturgy and Culture' in *Liturgy in Dialogue*, Paul F. Bradshaw and B. Spinks, eds. (SPCK, 1994), p. 49.

39. Robin Gill, *Moral Communities* (University of Exeter, 1992), p. 81.

40. Daniel Hardy and David Ford, *Praising and Knowing God* (Westminster, 1985), p. 19.

41. Walker, op. cit., p. 198.

42. Q magazine on the success of Orthodox composer John Tavener.

43. Faithless, 'God is a DJ', *Sunday 8PM* (Cheeky Records, 1998).

44. Richard Benson, editor of *The Face*, in *The Guardian*.

45. Simon Reynolds, *Energy Flash* (Picador, 1998), p. xix.

46. David le Jars, *The Big Issue*.

47. Desmond Tutu, *Hope and Suffering* (Fount, 1983), pp. 134–135.

48. Ford, op. cit., p. 145.

49. Gill, op. cit., p. 23.

50. Anthony Thiselton, *Interpreting God and the Postmodern Self*

(T.&T. Clark, 1995), p. 154f.

51. For the philosophical contrast between these two views,
see Paul Ricoeur, *Oneself as Another* (University of
Chicago, 1992), pp. 4–16.

52. Christopher Lasch, *The Minimal Self* (Norton, 1984).

53. Anthony Giddens, *Modernity and Self-identity* (Stanford
University Press, 1991), p. 5.

54. Zygmunt Bauman, *Life in Fragments* (Blackwell, 1995),
p. 81.

55. This is the primary point of David Ford's *Self and
Salvation*.

56. Gill, op. cit., pp. 55f.

57. Ford, op. cit., pp. 164f.

DOING THE STORY

1. William James, 'The Varieties of Religious Experience:
A Study in Human Nature', *The Gifford Lectures on Natural
Religion delivered in Edinburgh 1901–2* (Collins, 1977).

2. This is the subtitle to *Religion in Britain Since 1945* by
Grace Davie (Blackwell, 1994).

3. This is the title of the study of attitudes to Christianity
during childhood and adolescence by William Kay and
Leslie Francis (University of Wales Press, 1996).

4. For discussion of these issues, see 'From Presley to
Tarantino' by John Allan in Dean Borgman and Chris
Cook, eds., *Agenda for Youth Ministry* (SPCK, 1998).

REFERENCES

5.   H. Jenkins, quoted in *Approaches to Popular Film*, J. Hollows and M. Jancovich, eds. (Manchester University Press, 1995).

6.   Walker, op. cit.

7.   An example of this is the story I mentioned earlier of the Oxford college porter—it was a friend of a friend of mine who rang the college for the times of the services. If you now repeat the story, it is because it has 'every-man' content. Most jokes that are stories fall into this category.

8.   Kenda Creasy Dean, 'X-Files and Unknown Gods: the search for truth of post-modern adolescents', paper presented at the Third International Youth Ministry Conference in Oxford, January 1999, p. 5.

9.   A saying famously attributed to Dorothy L. Sayers.

10. For example, M. White and D. Epston, *Narrative Means to Therapeutic Ends* (Norton, 1990), and the body of narrative research among marginalized people.

11. G. Loughlin, *Telling God's Story: Bible, Church and Narrative Theology* (Cambridge University Press, 1996), p. 18.

12. Gordon Lynch and David Willows, *Telling Tales: The Narrative Dimension of Pastoral Care and Counselling* (Contact Pastoral Monograph No. 8, 1998), pp. 23–24.

13. See, for example, Peter Berger and Thomas Luckmann, *The Social Construction of Reality* (Penguin, 1979).

14. Lesslie Newbigin, *The Gospel in a Pluralist Society* (SPCK, 1994), ch. 19.

15. Oxford Youth Works, the para-Church organization that I have the privilege of working within, seeks to be a

mission community, with worship as an intrinsic part of its life, interwoven with its mission among young people.

16. Notably within some sections of the Church of England, following a Bishops' ruling that this could be decided at a parish level. Similarly, some new churches include children in 'breaking bread'.

17. This was related by a professional storyteller at a day workshop on storytelling at the Pitt Rivers Museum in Oxford in 1995.

CHARISMA, FREEDOM AND THE EUCHARIST

1. John Leach, *Living Liturgy* (Kingsway, 1997), p. 54.

2. ibid., p. 64.

3. Robert E. Webber, *Blended Worship* (Hendrickson Peabody, 1996), p. 46.

4. ibid.

5. Patrick Angier, *Changing Youth Worship* (National Society/ Church House Publishing, 1997).

6. ibid.

7. *Patterns for Worship* (Church House Publishing, 1995).

8. Eleanor Kreider, *Given for You* (Inter-Varsity Press, 1998), p. 77.

9. Webber, op. cit., p. 142.

10. Derek Brown, *Bread and Wine* (Sovereign World, 1998),

REFERENCES

pp. 17–18.

11. Alan Palmer, *Declare His Glory* (Paternoster, 1998), p. 76.

12. Chris Seaton and Roger Ellis, *New Celts* (Kingsway, 1998), p. 150.

13. Webber, op. cit., p. 64.

14. Brown, op. cit., p. 10.

15. Robert E. Webber, *Renew Your Worship* (Hendrickson Peabody, 1996), p. 65.

16. Webber, *Blended Worship*, p. 103.

17. Palmer, op. cit., p. 76.

18. Robert E. Webber, *Rediscovering the Missing Jewel* (Hendrickson Peabody, 1996), p. 114.